The Edible Ornamental Garden

D1151045

By John E. Bryan & Coralie Castle

PITMAN PUBLISHING

Illustrations reproduced from *Gerard's Herbal* (1633)
Courtesy Helen Crocker Russell Library of Horticulture,
Strybing Arboretum Society, San Francisco;
and from old French and English botanical books
from the private collection of John E. Bryan.
Illustrations, pages 58, 76, 77, 86: Sara Raffetto.
Plot Plans: C. Hannum

First published in the United States 1974
First published in Great Britain 1976

Pitman Limited
Pitman House, 39 Parker Street, London WC2B 5PB

Sir Isaac Pitman and Sons Limited
Banda Street, P.O. Box 46038, Nairobi, Kenya

Pitman Publishing Co. S.A. (Pty) Limited
Craighall Mews, Jan Smuts Avenue, Craighall Park, Johannesburg 2001, South Africa

This edition has been adapted for British readers by Anthony Huxley and Helena
Radecka from the original publication by 101 Publications, San Francisco.

ISBN: 0 273 00098 5

Text set in 11/13 pt IBM Press Roman, printed by photolithography,
and bound in Great Britain at The Pitman Press, Bath

Contents

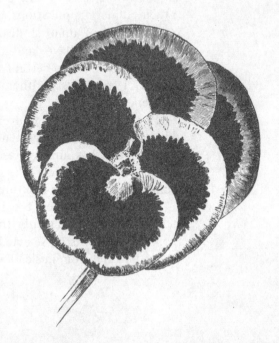

Preface

Historically, man first cultivated plants for sustenance. As food became more plentiful, he began to cultivate wild plants for their ornamental qualities, too. The aristocracy, utilizing peasants' expertise, developed fabulous gardens from Babylon to Versailles. Then, as flower and tree culture expanded through the years, colorful flowers and decorative trees found their way into the tiniest gardens.

Of course, growing plants for food has never lost its importance, but except for certain fruit trees, edible plants have traditionally been separated from the ornamental garden.

Here we propose a unique approach: commonly known edible plants, lesser known for their decorative qualities, blended with ornamental flowers, bushes and trees almost completely unknown today for their culinary applications, along with unusual recipes for both.

All sorts of unusual dishes are possible when ornamentals are explored for their flavor and aroma as food, many uses of which are buried in history. As certain plants were developed specifically for food, edible portions of others more notable for their eye-appeal were forgotten.

Here we bring to your attention a number of plants with a culinary history and suggest new ones, not in the wilderness where recent interest has already resulted in numerous books, but in your own garden where you like to work, relax and entertain, where familiar plants can play exciting new roles.

We have designated the species and varieties in this book, and would recommend that only these be used for culinary purposes. It is, essential that plants be selected by Latin names, not common names, as the latter are often misleading, varying from region to region.

John E. Bryan and Coralie Castle

Weights and Measures

The recipes in this book were originally devised and tested using American cup and spoon measures. These have been converted to fractions of pounds, ounces and pints where it seemed most practical. However, in some cases, where comparative volumes are more important to the success of a dish, the original cup measures have been retained.

The American cup holds 8 fluid ounces, the equivalent of a medium-sized teacup, and 2 cups, or 16 fluid ounces, make 1 American pint. (The Imperial pint holds 20 fluid ounces, or one-fifth more, and whenever pints have been used it is the 20-ounce pint that is meant.) However, provided the same cup is used throughout a recipe, a slight discrepancy will not matter. What is important is that cups, tablespoons and teaspoons should always be measured level.

For those who wish to use metric measures, the equivalents, adjusted to the nearest convenient figure, are as follows (volume and weight).

Should you wish to make a more accurate conversion (particularly useful for baking, etc.), the exact equivalents are:

1 ounce	=	28.35 grammes
16 ounces	=	453.6 grammes
1 pint	=	568 millilitres
1 kilo	=	2.2 pounds
1 litre	=	1.76 pints
1 decilitre	=	100 millilitres

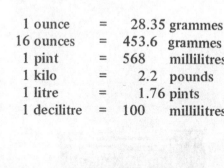

OUNCES/FLUID OUNCES		GRAMMES/MILLILITRES
½	=	15
1	=	25
2	=	50
3	=	75
4 (¼ pound)	=	100–110
5 (¼ pint)	=	150 (1½ decilitres)
6	=	175
7	=	200 (2 decilitres)
8 (½ pound)	=	225 (use ¼ kilo)
9	=	250 (2½ decilitres = ¼ kilo)
10 (½ pint)	=	275 (use 2½ decilitres)
11	=	300 (3 decilitres)
12	=	350 (3½ decilitres)
13	=	375
14	=	400 (4 decilitres)
15 (¾ pint)	=	425 (4½ decilitres)
16 (1 pound)	=	450 (4½ decilitres)
17	=	475
18	=	500 (5 decilitres = ½ kilo)
19	=	550 (5½ decilitres)
20 (1 pint)	=	575 (use 5½ decilitres)

The oven temperatures in this book are given in °F. Gas Regulo and Celsius (Centigrade) equivalents are as follows:

	FAHRENHEIT		GAS MARK		CELSIUS
very cool	225	=	¼	=	110
very cool	250	=	½	=	130
cool	275	=	1	=	140
very slow	300	=	2	=	150
slow	325	=	3	=	160
moderate	350	=	4	=	180
moderate	375	=	5	=	190
moderately hot	400	=	6	=	200
fairly hot	425	=	7	=	220
hot	450	=	8	=	230
very hot	475	=	9	=	240
extremely hot	500	=	10	=	250

General Culture of Plants

EARTH.—Earth may be divided into three classes, sandy, loamy, and clayey.

A good garden Earth may be either of a blackish, hazelly; or chesnut-brown colour neither too light loose and sandy, nor partake too much of loam or clay, but is fattish, light pliant, and easy to work at all seasons; and if three spades deep, it will be still more beneficial for the purpose, though if there be eighteen inches or two feet depth of good staple, it will do for most sorts of esculent plants, and others, as well as for almost all sorts of fruit trees.

Sandy Earth.—All the light, loose, open, and gravelly soils, whether black, grey, hazelly, or yellowish coloured, till the loam or clay is come at, may be deemed of the sandy kind, and is capable of raising some certain plants; but having a mixture of loam or clay, and enriched with dung, it will produce all sorts; for a vegetable planted either in sand alone, or in a fat coherent glebe or Earth alone, receives scarce any growth, but where there is a just mixture of both, the mass becomes fertile.

By means of sand or sandy Earth, strong loam or clay is fertilized, the Earth being thereby rendered porous, and interstices or space maintained, by which the juices are prepared, and thrown off into the roots of the plants, and the fibres finds room to extend themselves.

Sandy or gravelly ground easily admits both of heat and moisture, and are apt to push feeds and plants much earlier in spring than strong loamy or clayey soils.

But sandy land is liable to these inconveniencies, that being sometimes very light and open, it either does not retain a due portion of moisture, or sometimes retains it too long, especially where there is clay at bottom; so in these cases, is apt either to parch or chill too much.

There have been many books written regarding the culture and care of individual plants, but certain general information is applicable to all plants. This information can be categorized under major headings based upon the normal sequence of operations from propagation to final establishment of the mature plant or tree, at which point only the general maintenance such as pruning, thinning, watering and spraying is involved.

SOIL

The text to the side, written 200 years ago in Mawes' *Encyclopedia of Gardening,* is a good summary of things we should remember about the earth. At the time, the main soil amendments available were dung and sand. Other materials are now recognized as necessary to provide nourishment, aeration, moisture balance and soil pest control.

Additions to the soil can be permanent, such as sand, or temporary, such as humus that breaks down with bacterial action. Soil bacteria require extra oxygen and nitrogen to break down straw and fresh sawdust or shavings, which will deprive growing plants of nutrients if they are not well rotted before application.

Porous soil, everyone knows, is essential if water is to penetrate. Lesser known is the need for roots to have available at least three percent (but not over five percent) oxygen and the importance of preventing stifling mineral accumulation around roots in heavy soil, which may cause burning of leaf tips.

Most plants reproduce by seeds, but this is by no means the only method of propagation. Runners are produced by strawberries, for example. Layers are another means of natural propagation. A branch of a tree or shrub in contact with the soil will frequently produce roots at the point of contact, and such branches once rooted, if separated from the parent plant and planted by themselves, will flourish. Several ferns produce small plantlets on the edges of their leaves which can be removed and easily grown.

A plant produced from seed is not necessarily identical to the parent plant. Both the male pollen which fertilized and the female flower assert their influence on progeny. It is by cross pollination of selected parents that hybridizers are able to produce many new plants which are different in color, form and habit. One need only compare seed catalogues of today with those of other years to see the improvements in many of our common vegetables and flowers.

Propagation by seeds is called sexual reproduction, while by other means it is called vegetative or asexual propagation. The advantage of the asexual method is that each plant produced is identical to its single parent, being in effect part of the original plant.

Germination

The many types of seeds can be broadly classified into six classes: dust-like, such as the begonia; hard coated, such as the rose, walnut and peach; fleshy, such as the sweet chestnut; oily, such as the magnolia; winged, such as the sycamore; or plumed, such as the dandelion.

Seeds need air, warmth and moisture to germinate. After germination, light is essential. A seed has been described as a wound-up clock, set in motion only when the above conditions are present. Air is essential for the biological and chemical changes which take place inside the seeds. Warmth is required to activate the life process inside the seed, the proper temperature being determined by the origin of the seeds. Plants from the tropics naturally require more heat than seeds from a temperate zone. Moisture is needed so that the seed coat

will soften, enabling the roots and stem to develop. The roots must quickly extract nutrients from the soil to supplement the food reserves within the seeds, and shoots must start manufacturing food from light and air for the plant to develop normally.

Sowing

Seeds vary tremendously in size from the mustard seed to the coconut. Much has been written about the depth of sowing seeds. A good rule to follow is to cover with soil proportionate in depth to the thickness of the seed. This means in some cases little covering at all; in others, planting one-quarter to one-half inch deep. Depending on the climate and season, seeds can be sown in the open garden, in a cold greenhouse or cold frame, or in a greenhouse where heat is available.

The seed beds should be well worked over and the soil brought to a fine tilth. This means there should be no stones, rocks or large clumps of earth. It may be necessary to pass the soil through a quarter-inch wire screen. The soil should contain well-rotted humus so that it can retain moisture, and should be aerated enough so that the seeds will not suffocate. Seeds may be either broadcast or sown in rows. If sowing in rows, make a trench of the depth desired with the back of a rake or by imprinting a fine board into the soil. Place the seeds in the trench, cover with earth and water in well with a soft gentle supply of water so as not to disturb the planted seeds.

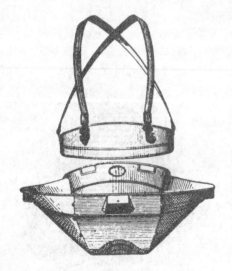

If the seeds are to be sown in a flat or pot, the container should be cleaned, and good drainage provided by placing pieces of broken pots, or if not available, sharp, coarse gravel over the holes in the bottom of the container. Fill the container with a mixture of soil containing two parts loam, one part moss peat and one part coarse builder's sand, well mixed. Firm with your finger tips and level the soil surface with a flat board. Sow the seed and cover with soil to the proper depth. Soaking pots in a bucket obviates disturbing the seeds with too heavy a spray of overhead watering. Label containers, and mark dates of sowing. Place containers in a warm place and do not allow to dry out. Many growers cover the containers with sheets of glass or clear plastic until germination takes place. Once germination has taken place, however, all coverings must be removed.

Cuttings

Many people do not understand exactly what is meant by the term "cutting." Simply stated, it is any vegetative part of a plant separated from a parent plant and treated in such a manner that it will grow into a new plant. The basic difference between a cutting and the division of a plant is that with division the new plant already has roots, stems and sometimes leaves so the division has no need to form these. A cutting, however, is an incomplete plant. While it may have leaves, it will not have roots; if a root cutting is made, it will lack stems and leaves. Any compost used for root cuttings should be made up of coarse builder's sand mixed with moss peat in an approximate proportion of three parts sand to one and a half parts peat. No fertilizers are required and good drainage is essential. It is beneficial to cover many cuttings with a clear plastic tent. For the small home garden, large glass jars placed over the pots are a successful way to construct a miniature greenhouse.

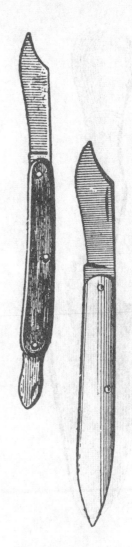

Cuttings of trees and shrubs can be either hard wood or soft wood. The hard-wood cuttings are made from growth of previous years detached from the parent plant during the winter months. Normally, they do not have a terminal bud, but are sections of the stem cut into lengths which can vary from 10 to 14 inches depending on the type of plant being propagated. The bottom cut should be made horizontally just below a node, the point where the leaves were attached. The top cut should be just above a node. It is important to cut close to a node because there is a greater concentration of cambium tissue which has the unique quality of being able to produce the callus (scar tissue) from which roots are produced.

Soft-wood cuttings are those taken during the current season's growth in early summer or late spring when the base of that growth has begun to harden, or lignify. Frequently, this hardening can be easily seen by the change in color of the shoot from light green to dark green or brown. Normally, soft-wood cuttings are shorter than hard-wood cuttings, rarely more than four or five inches in length.

Once taken, stem cuttings should have the lower leaves removed so that the part inserted into the compost (approximately one-half the length) is without leaves. Firm well and water. Hard-wood cuttings

11

should be placed in an area which is not exposed to full sun. They will normally be selected in November or December; after one year they will be well rooted. Depending upon the vigor of the plant, they can either be planted into a permanent place in the garden, potted in a container, or lined into rows for another season before final planting.

Soft-wood cuttings should be protected by plastic, as there is a great loss of moisture from the softer leaves and stems which will cause them to dehydrate before roots develop to extract sufficient moisture from the compost. They prefer a soil temperature of approximately 55° F.

Certain plants have the ability to propagate from root cuttings. Root sections of approximately pencil thickness are cut into four- or five-inch lengths. These are buried in the compost with the top of the cutting barely below the surface. To keep the right side up, make a horizontal cut at the top and a slanting cut at the base to facilitate planting of the cuttings.

Some plants can produce plantlets from leaves. The procedure is to take a leaf, slit the main veins, peg the leaf into a sandy mixture and keep moist. Plantlets will form at the cut edges of the vein. Certain begonias are an example of plants with such capability.

After planting, cuttings should always be kept moist but never too wet. This especially applies to soft-wood cuttings. Normally, hard-wood cuttings inserted outdoors require no more than the initial watering. Once rooted, soft-wood cuttings should be potted in a light soil mixture containing loam, sand and moss peat in equal parts. There are many commercial rooting mixes on the market today, but while most are excellent, it is advisable to add sand to make them lighter for freshly rooted cuttings.

Dip cuttings in hormone rooting powder, following the maker's instructions, especially with woody plants.

PLANTING

Planting or transplanting a tree, shrub or flower is one of the gardener's most rewarding experiences, though it can be devastating later if the plant dies or performs poorly. Often, disappointment is the result of neglecting basic rules.

It is best to plant in early autumn or to wait until spring. Before planting, position the container on the ground and consider the following: space for growth (usually much more than a young plant seems to deserve); a harmonious relation with other nearby plants with respect to flower and foliage color; time of flowering; height; shade or wind protection; watering needs; and care during growth. A mistake sometimes made is placing plants requiring heavy feeding near those that need little, with wasteful results or undesired proliferous growth of the less hungry plants.

Think of future pruning. Will you be able to reach around the plant without wrestling with dense adjacent growth? Consider whether spraying can be done without harming nearby plants or fine paint surfaces on your house when selective strong insecticides must be used. The golden rule of planting is "Dig a £1 hole for a 50p plant." In other words, dig a more-than-adequate hole. You can easily refill it and chances are the extra volume of loosened soil will hasten root development. The hole's diameter and depth should be at least one and a half times those of the root ball of the plant, and its shape should be cylindrical, not bowl shaped. When digging near grass or ground covers, spread a plastic sheet to cut cleaning and to aid in replacing poor soil with compost and good top soil. After digging an adequate hole, fork over bottom and sides and mix in compost. A spade should not be used; it could glaze the sides and inhibit moisture distribution and root growth.

Remove plant from its container and loosen the root ball so the roots can spread. The habits developed in the pot are not always easily forgotten, and roots sometimes continue to grow in a circular pattern until they strangle the plant. Damaged roots should be cut off and branches should be lightly pruned immediately to compensate. Place the plant in the hole, stand back and check for depth (the same as in

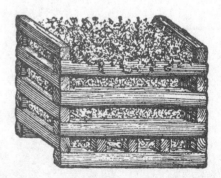

the container), vertical alignment and orientation of branch structure for future development. If the plant needs staking, follow the instructions given below. Fill in the hole with good soil, tamping carefully and maintaining alignment. Water well and add more soil in a few days if settling has occurred. Keep moist until plant shows it is established, then revert to normal watering for the species.

If planting bare-root plants, allow space in the hole for the roots to spread. While filling the hole and before tamping, shake these plants gently so that the soil will fill in around the roots. Then water in well.

For a plant that needs staking, place the stake close to the ball or main stem on the least conspicuous side without interfering with major roots; drive in well *before* filling the hole. Tamp around the stake after filling to increase its stability and tie the plant to it with soft, thick twine or wire threaded through lengths of soft hose. Label the plant, especially if it is unfamiliar.

Winds can sometimes disturb new plantings, allowing too much air to get at the roots and causing dehydration. A little extra tamped-in soil and water will quickly remedy this.

Don't fertilize newly transplanted trees, flowers and shrubs until they show growth in the spring. Roots are then better able to absorb stronger food.

If evergreens or plants with leaves are moved, keep the foliage as well as the roots moist to create an individual "microclimate." Watering foliage is a good rule for all plants during dry summers. Accumulated dust cuts down the absorption of vital light needed for photosynthesis, the process by which plants utilize air, light, nutrients and moisture for essential life functions.

If the careful gardener not only plants well, but also constantly examines his plants to see if they need extra care, his efforts will be well rewarded.

CARE OF ESTABLISHED PLANTS

Most established plants don't need pampering, but they do require reasonable, knowledgeable care. The enthusiastic gardener may bog down unless he develops efficiency in providing continuing needs such as water, food, space and protection from weeds and pests, but he should tackle the essentials with enjoyment and relaxation in mind.

To retain moisture and inhibit weed growth, mulch bare ground after removing weeds, especially those with deep roots such as docks and thistles. Apply pre-emergent herbicide to prevent weed seed germination. Place a layer of chopped branches and leaves, bark chips, moss peat, straw, sawdust, lawn clippings, gravel or small stones, though not so thick as to keep air and moisture from the ground. Avoid plastic sheets, as they cause the ground to sweat and sour.

A ground cover of low plants to be used in the kitchen can serve in place of a mulch. Chamomile, thyme, strawberry and mint add more beauty to the garden than inert mulches. Stepping stones or wood roundels should protect this plant cover from heavy traffic. Remember to keep ground covers trimmed away from the primary plants so they won't steal all the water.

Bare soil areas should be raked level in the spring, then cultivated to a depth of three inches. Even though no weeds appear, repeat as necessary after watering, keeping a fine layer of dust on the surface to hold down evaporation and prevent weed seeds from germinating.

Watering

Both excess and insufficient watering can be damaging. Know your plant's needs, your soil (both the surface and subsurface), and evaluate exposure to heat and wind. Remember plants in pots and planter boxes lose moisture more quickly than those in the ground.

Roots tend to grow toward moisture. Light watering is not suitable except for shallow-rooted plants. All others should be watered deeply (and less frequently) until it is obvious no further penetration is being achieved. If soil is unusually heavy, it may be necessary to punch holes near plants in the spring and fill them with fine gravel to allow water to penetrate deeply during the summer.

Feeding

Most plants require feeding at least twice a year, in the spring for growth (nitrogen) and in late summer to harden the wood for winter (phosphorus and potassium). Light soils and planted boxes require more frequent feeding because nutrients tend to leach out; heavier soils retain them to the extent that it is possible to damage plants by overfeeding. Because all plant foods are labelled by content (N, nitrogen; P, phosphorus; K, potassium), selection of the proper one with the help of a nurseryman is relatively simple.

Overfeeding by the anxious gardener can harm a healthy plant. Well-rooted manure, moss peat and compost, well dug in during winter or spring, are most beneficial in moderation. Prepared fertilizers, generally more concentrated, must be used sparingly, following the manufacturer's instructions.

Fertilize according to needs. Always water first, apply the fertilizer, then water again. To avoid burning, fertilizer must reach the roots well diluted and should be soaked in rather than remain on the surface, where sunlight may break it down or generate chemical fumes injurious to leaves.

Soil Problems

Common soil problems are too much acidity (treat with lime), too much alkalinity (treat with sulphur) or an excess of salts. Raised beds will allow such chemical imbalances to dissipate.

Iron deficiency shows up in chlorosis of the leaves (leaves turn yellow while veins stay green) and calls for iron sulphate or chelates. Sometimes excess alkalinity prevents the plant from utilizing available iron. Soil analysis will aid in determining what fertilizer your soil needs to overcome inherent imbalances. There are do-it-yourself soil-analysing kits available which are particularly useful if you wish to measure the relative acidity/alkalinity of the soil.

PRUNING

Since volumes have been published about pruning, it may seem presumptuous to tackle such a complicated subject in a short section such as this. However, the basic principles are straightforward. No one needs to approach pruning with fear and trepidation if certain rules are followed. Anyone can become proficient with experience.

Pruning is necessary to:

- Produce a well-balanced plant (be it shrub or tree) that is neither top-heavy nor growing only in one direction.
- Promote the formation of more fruit or flowers.
- Give air and light to the center of the plant.
- Shape into desirable conformations.
- Prevent overcrowding.
- Eliminate potential wind damage or danger to passers-by from falling branches.

Get acquainted with each plant and learn its growth, flowering and fruit-bearing characteristics. If the plant produces flowers on the previous year's branches, prune to leave as many as possible; if it flowers on new growth, encourage that wood by shortening old branches. For spur-flowering and fruiting plants such as apple trees, stop the forward growth to produce laterals. Shoots are either leaders, growing upward, or laterals, growing away from a branch. Unless damaged, leaders and main shoots of young plants should be left untouched until they reach the desired height at which you want branches to form.

If a shrub gets crowded, thin out the center, but leave a good form. To keep such a plant within bounds, remove one third of the growth each year, or a quarter of the growth every four years.

If a plant flowers in the early spring, prune after flowering so it can produce summer wood for the following spring's bloom. For late-flowering species, pruning in autumn permits early shaping of the next summer's branches.

Where to prune? Just above where a leaf joins the stem or where a side branch grows. Always prune cautiously, stepping back frequently to get an overall look. Branches should be well spaced around

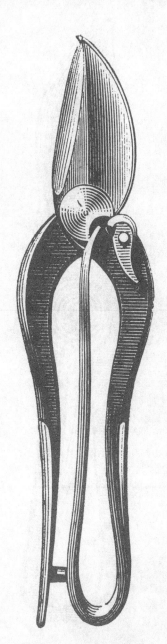

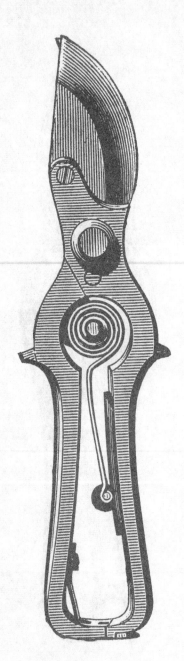

the trunk, not rise from the same height on the stem, or angle too severely from trunks or main branches. It is best to keep your wits about you, cutting moderately first then more drastically if required as you observe the results. Like a sculptor, the accomplished pruner starts with a whole and produces a thing of beauty by carefully removing just the right material. He can't add leaves and branches to cover mistakes like an artist piling oil colors on a canvas. True, he can paint over large cuts, but this is simply a cosmetic approach serving no other purpose, for the plant usually heals itself.

Specific examples may provide further insights into the art of pruning. Fuchsias flower on new wood, so prune severely in the spring, thin out weak branches and form a good structure.

Apple trees bear fruit on spurs. Remove dead and damaged wood first. Next cut out all crossing or rubbing branches. To produce more laterals, cut side branches just beyond eight or nine buds. The last or top three will produce long shoots, the others fruit-bearing spurs. Repeat each year, being careful to leave all spurs intact. Random shoots arising from thicker branches are not part of the main structure and should be removed completely during the dormant season along with suckers around the base.

Pruning of evergreens can be done at any time. Special care should be taken not to misshape the tree, and cutting should be back to a lateral or a hidden point where it does not affect the beauty of the tree.

Root pruning should only be done if it is unavoidable. It involves digging a trench around the plant and cutting far-ranging roots that may interfere with surrounding plants. A more compact root structure will then result.

With these basic requirements in mind the average gardener can approach pruning with confidence and derive great satisfaction from his artistry.

DISEASES, DISORDERS AND PESTS

Just as the hypochondriac is sometimes overwhelmed by human ailments, the worried gardener can dwell unduly on the vast array of plant enemies. It is no more necessary, however, to study all the tomes on plant diseases than it is to read through medical encyclopedias. As with pruning, the alert gardener learns certain protective and corrective strategies, turns to knowledgeable local nurserymen and agricultural specialists for help and uses reputable commercial products with explicit instructions to solve specific problems.

Diseases are caused by bacteria, viruses or fungi. The animal and insect worlds swarm with creatures eager to devour your favorite plants. Chemical imbalance in the soil can cause disorders. Soil structure and moisture availability can be unsuitable. It is necessary to recognize the enemy and act promptly.

Before using chemical sprays, try simple controls such as spraying with cold water, soapy water or a garlic spray. To make a garlic spray, grind in the blender, with a little water, one chopped onion, one teaspoon cayenne pepper, three garlic cloves; add four cups of water. Let stand 24 hours and strain through a stocking. This is particularly effective on aphids and white flies. If no control is achieved by these natural means, use a mild commercial spray, specifically listed as safe for food crops, following directions carefully. Do not harvest within the specified period after spraying and be sure to wash everything well before eating if you have used chemicals in your garden.

Bacteria

One of the common bacterial diseases is fireblight, which attacks apple, pear, pyracantha and quince, and gets its name from causing a limb to appear as if seared by great heat. The whole shoot suddenly becomes limp and withers. Though streptomycin spray has been used in the U.S., it is not recommended in Britain, and a Ministry of Agriculture order requires infected trees to be cut down and burned without delay.

Viruses

Virus diseases produce abnormal growth (sometimes pretty in color) and are transmitted by insects. There is no cure except surgical removal and disposal of the infected plant. To prevent spreading, aphids, thrips and white flies must be kept from chewing the infected plant and transfering its sap to a healthy one. Controlling weeds and allowing free air passage will also help.

Fungi

Mildew: This familiar grey or white covering spreads primarily in humid weather or shady, moist areas and is inhibited by free air passage. If it becomes a problem, a nurseryman can recommend a good spray.

Rust: A rust-colored fungus which usually grows on the undersides of leaves and spreads by water and wind. Cleaning up debris in the winter and keeping the garden weed free will help, but a special spray may be needed.

Botrytis or Grey Mould: Attacks suddenly and may require prompt spraying and removal of debris and infected branches. Also, spraying of the debris or compost helps to destroy harbored spores.

Leaf Spots: Dark spots which appear on the leaves; spray with fungicide and remove badly attacked limbs.

Pests

The principal groups are leaf chewers, sucking pests, soil pests and burrowers.

Leaf Chewers: Snails and slugs are controlled by commercial bait or by using upright empty grapefruit halves to attract them and then using a heavy foot. Earwig bait is also available. Or trap by placing an upside-down flower pot filled with straw on a stake; earwigs congregate in such areas. Destroy straw with entrapped earwigs. Caterpillars, grasshoppers or moths require spraying. Frequent checking and early treatment is most effective, though it is poor practice to overspray or spray before pests are observed in action.

Sucking Pests: Malathion spray can control the following: Spider mites (leaf silvering or webs they form), thrips (rasp plant surfaces), white flies (which can be controlled by cold fine-mist water spraying), mealy bugs and their colonies at leaf and stem joints, and aphids (black, yellow, green or pink).

Soil Pests: Since soil pests such as wireworms, grubs and symphilids attack subsurface stems and roots, the first symptom may be sudden wilting of a healthy-looking plant. Before they spread, lift the affected plant carefully with its roots onto a newspaper and examine closely for pests and damage. Soaking with chlordane solution is often the answer, but your nurseryman with his experience may recommend other treatment.

Burrowers: Leaf miners and stem borers, which are larvae of some moths, eat leaf or stem tissue, causing a lace-like effect. The trick is to kill the adults before the larvae enter or, in small attacks, to pick off the damaged leaves and stems.

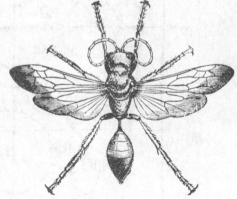

PLANTING SCHEME FOR VARYING-SIZED GARDEN SPACES

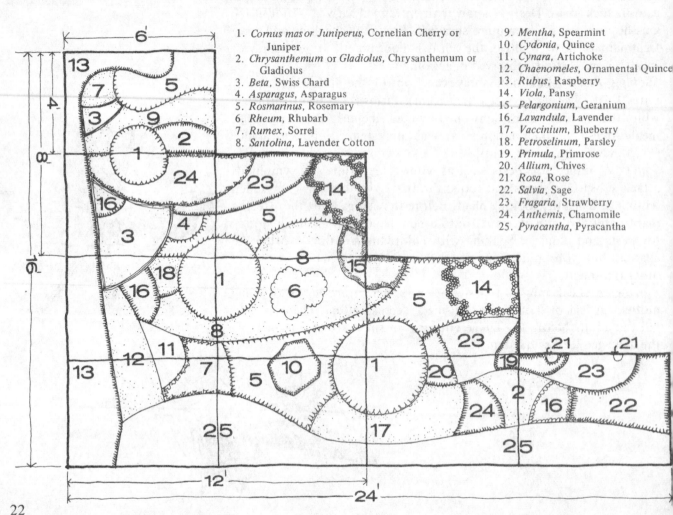

1. *Cornus mas* or *Juniperus*, Cornelian Cherry or Juniper
2. *Chrysanthemum* or *Gladiolus*, Chrysanthemum or Gladiolus
3. *Beta*, Swiss Chard
4. *Asparagus*, Asparagus
5. *Rosmarinus*, Rosemary
6. *Rheum*, Rhubarb
7. *Rumex*, Sorrel
8. *Santolina*, Lavender Cotton
9. *Mentha*, Spearmint
10. *Cydonia*, Quince
11. *Cynara*, Artichoke
12. *Chaenomeles*, Ornamental Quince
13. *Rubus*, Raspberry
14. *Viola*, Pansy
15. *Pelargonium*, Geranium
16. *Lavandula*, Lavender
17. *Vaccinium*, Blueberry
18. *Petroselinum*, Parsley
19. *Primula*, Primrose
20. *Allium*, Chives
21. *Rosa*, Rose
22. *Salvia*, Sage
23. *Fragaria*, Strawberry
24. *Anthemis*, Chamomile
25. *Pyracantha*, Pyracantha

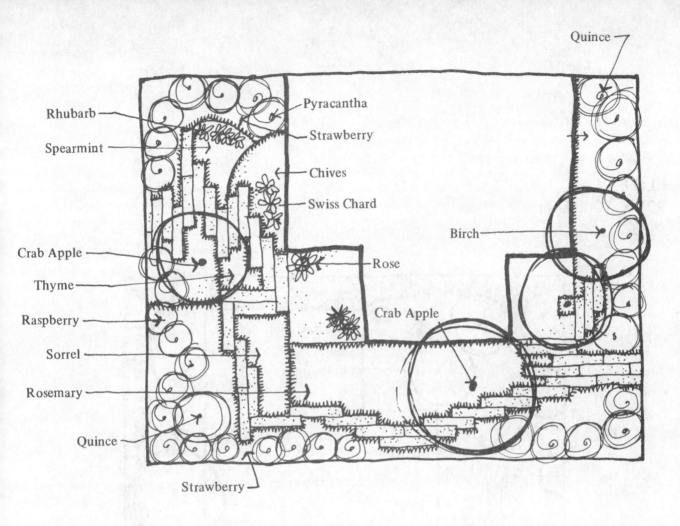

Rhubarb
Pyracantha
Spearmint
Strawberry
Chives
Swiss Chard
Crab Apple
Thyme
Rose
Raspberry
Crab Apple
Sorrel
Rosemary
Quince
Quince
Birch
Strawberry

PLOT PLAN
60' X 75' LOT

23

PLOT PLAN
90' X 100' LOT

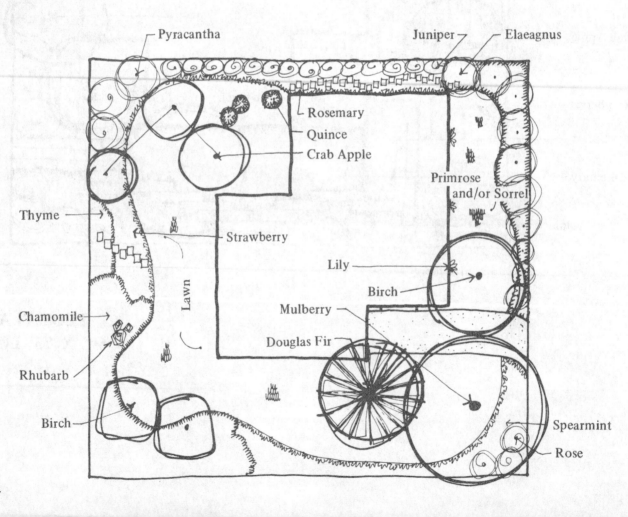

Pyracantha

Juniper

Elaeagnus

Rosemary

Quince

Crab Apple

Primrose and/or Sorrel

Thyme

Strawberry

Lily

Chamomile

Birch

Mulberry

Rhubarb

Douglas Fir

Lawn

Birch

Spearmint

Rose

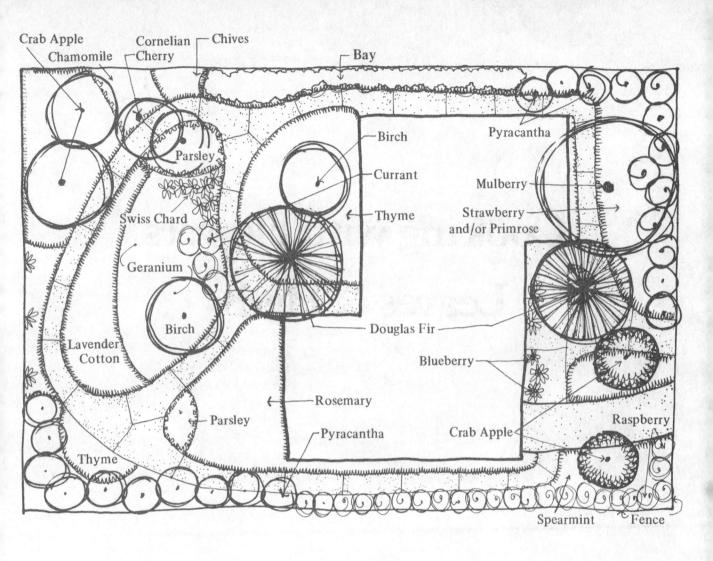

Crab Apple
Chamomile
Cornelian Cherry
Chives
Bay
Pyracantha
Birch
Currant
Mulberry
Thyme
Strawberry and/or Primrose
Parsley
Swiss Chard
Geranium
Birch
Douglas Fir
Lavender Cotton
Blueberry
Rosemary
Raspberry
Parsley
Pyracantha
Crab Apple
Thyme
Spearmint
Fence

**PLOT PLAN
100' X 150' LOT**

Cooking with Flowers
Leaves & Herbs

When using this book as a guide to edible plants, be sure to eat only those plants of the same botanical name; do not confuse the plants included here with others having the same common name. Other edible flowers may be substituted for ones called for in the recipes. When harvesting, be careful of any use of harmful sprays and insect damage on the plants. Use vegetables, berries and flowers as soon as possible after gathering; gather seeds in the early stage of ripening. The strength of herbs will vary with the maturity of the leaves.

FLOWERS, LEAVES AND HERBS

Gather flowers, leaves and herbs before the sun is on them. Wash gently, dry thoroughly and wrap in paper towelling. To dry, hang or place them in a single layer on fine mesh and let dry in a warm, dark, dust-free area. When dry, store whole, crumbled or pulverized (sieved) in an airtight glass container in a dark place. In recipes calling for fresh flowers or herbs, substitute half the amount if using dried.

To Make Syrup: Boil one cup water, three cups sugar and the desired amount of petals or herbs 10 minutes, or until syrupy. Strain through cheesecloth, seal and store up to two weeks.

To Make Honey: Chop fresh or crush dried petals or herbs and add them to a jar of mild honey. Cover jar, place in gently boiling water and simmer 30 minutes. Remove from water bath and cool. Store one week before using; strain if desired.

To Make Oil: Follow directions for making honey using vegetable oil. In the case of garlic-flavored oil, mentioned in a number of recipes, it is not necessary to put it in a water bath. Simply add three or four crushed garlic cloves to a pint of olive oil and let stand at least four days before using. If not used up in two weeks, strain out the garlic. Remember that the strength of any flavored oil will depend on how long it stands before it is strained.

To Make Tea: Steep one to three teaspoons of petals or leaves (usually dried) for each cup of hot water, three to 10 minutes or to taste. In some cases, the flavor is enhanced by combining with black tea.

To Make Vinegar: Pour room-temperature vinegar over petals or herbs, fresh or dried, cover and let stand in a warm area for one week. Strain through cheesecloth and store in a cool place.

To Infuse Stock: Simmer any kind of stock with fresh or dried herbs, leaves, flowers or petals, until infused with flavor to taste.

To Make Butter: Layer softened butter and chopped petals or herbs in a container. Cover and refrigerate one week or more.

FLOWERS

Discard stamen and sepal and remove the appendage attached to the base of the flower. Use as a garnish, to add color and texture, for salads, vegetables, meats, sauces or as recipes and suggestions indicate. For salads or as toppings, crisp fresh petals in ice water first. Use only enamel, glass or steel containers and wooden spoons when cooking flowers. Most flower petals called for in recipes may be substituted with others included in this book.

To Pickle Flowers: Layer flowers or buds in a glass or ceramic container, covering each layer with sugar. Add boiling cider or white vinegar to cover, and drop in a small piece of mace. Seal and store at least four days before using.

To Make Flower Sugar: Pound sugar and minced petals in a mortar. Cover and let stand one week. Sift, if desired, and store in an airtight container.

To Make Rose or Violet Water: The delicate aroma and flavor of fresh rose or violet petals can be captured into an essence at home by using an improvised still consisting of a large kettle with a sizeable lid and a three-foot length of thin flexible plastic tubing. Fill one third of the kettle with water, add as many washed petals as possible and bring to a gentle simmer. Insert the plastic tube in the spout just far enough to collect the vapors but not too far or the boiling water will be sucked into the tube. The tube should extend from the kettle through a shallow pan filled with ice cubes and water, to cool and condense the vapor. It should finally empty into a jar placed at a lower level, on the floor or a stool. Do not collect more than one cup of rose water from each batch or it will be too diluted.

To Deep Fry Flowers: Dip flowers or petals in batter (page 30) and deep fry in corn or peanut oil until golden. Drain and sprinkle with sugar or melted butter.

To Make Flower Fritters: Add as many flowers or petals to batter (page 30) as it will hold. Fry as you would pancakes.

FRUIT JUICE

Boil fruit, with as little water as necessary, until soft. Strain through a jelly bag. Add sugar to taste and spices, if desired, and cook until sugar is dissolved and flavors are blended.

CRYSTALLIZING LEAVES, FRUIT AND FLOWERS

Pick a non-humid day for crystallizing. Gather leaves, fruit or flowers after the sun has dried them and wipe clean. A feather brush works well for coating with egg white or syrup; use tongs or tweezers for dipping into syrup and then sugar. Several methods can be used:

• Paint with egg white beaten frothy and dip in castor sugar.
• Beat egg white until frothy and beat in icing sugar to make a coating consistency. Coat, place on a wire rack and sprinkle with castor sugar.
• Cook one cup sugar, one-half cup water and a dash of cream of tartar to thread stage. Dip into mixture and coat with castor sugar.
• Dissolve two ounces powdered gum arabic (stocked by some chemists) in three-quarters of a pint hot water. Cool. Dip into mixture and coat with castor sugar. This method keeps better than the others.
• If you want more color, add food coloring to syrup before coating flowers. After coating, place flowers, fruit or leaves, not touching, on fine wire mesh or wax paper. Dry in a warm area such as an unheated gas oven with the door open. When thoroughly dry, pack between wax paper in an airtight tin. Store up to three or four weeks.

BATTER
(For Dipping or Fritters)

In blender, mix:
1/4 pint flat beer, white wine, milk, coconut milk or milk in which flowers or herbs have been infused
2 eggs
5 ounces unbleached flour
1 teaspoon baking powder
1/2 teaspoon sugar (optional)
1/4 teaspoon salt
Cover and refrigerate at least 2 hours.

GLAZING FRUIT, FLOWERS AND LEAVES

In a lightweight saucepan, combine:
1 pound sugar
1/2 pint water
1/4 teaspoon cream of tartar
Stir over low heat to dissolve sugar. Then cook quickly, without stirring, until syrup reaches 280° (hard crack test). Quickly place pan in ice water to stop cooking. If desired, stir in:
4 drops lemon, lime or orange juice
Place pan over hot water to keep syrup from hardening and, working quickly, dip:
flowers, petals, leaves or fruit
into the syrup. Place on baking sheets to dry.

Plants: Their History
Culture & Recipes

Artichoke

(Cynara scolymus and cultivars)

ARTICHOKE
Cynara scolymus *and cultivars*
Herbaceous perennial
4 to 5 feet in height
Fast grower
Propagate from offshoots
Sun
Will not stand hard frost
Plants need 2 years to establish
Flower heads eaten
Harvest in spring and summer
Blue-purple flowers, gray foliage

The artichoke, one of the few plants with sizeable edible flower heads, has an interesting yet imprecisely recorded history. Believed by most authorities to be native to the western Mediterranean region and North Africa, it was grown in Egypt as early as 600 B.C. Its common name derives from the Ligurian (early inhabitants of what is now the Swiss-Italian border) word *cocali,* meaning cone, and the northern Italian name, *articolis.* In ancient Rome its highly prized leaves were used in salads and as a potherb. It is only in comparatively recent times that the flower heads have been eaten as well.

The artichoke was introduced to England in the 16th century. Gardens featured the ornamental beauty of the artichoke's dark-green to purplish-grey spiny foliage. Today the plant is quite widely grown for the production of edible artichokes, especially in milder areas, as well as an ornamental herbaceous perennial. One needs only allow the purple blossom to open to realize it is a spectacular oversized thistle.

The two basic types of this plant which are eaten today have been in existence since the early 16th century. These are the conical and the globular forms, the names of which refer to the shape of the heads. They vary in color from light green to purplish. Early plants had many spines on the tips of the leaves which made up the flower head, while today the spineless varieties are more popular.

While you can raise artichoke plants from seed, they will not come true from seed. That is, they will not be exactly the same as the parent plant. Propagation is easy and more predictable from the suckers which appear at the base of the plant. These suckers should be removed from the parent plant in March with a portion of the root structure attached. Plant them about two feet apart in well-drained soil, rich in humus, preferably in full sun. A top dressing of compost and copious watering of established plants should promote bushy growth to five feet within three years. Edible artichokes are not produced in quantity until the second or third year.

Pruning in the ordinary sense is not necessary, though severe cutting back is often desirable after each peak growing season. Feed well in the spring with a general garden fertilizer, keep weeds away from the collar of the plant to prevent rot and spray for aphids and earwigs if necessary. In colder climates where moderate ground freezing occurs, protect roots with straw or other cover. Artichokes are not long-lived and may require replacing (or drastic separating) every four or five years to maintain good production.

Despite precautions, home-grown artichokes are apt to have earwigs or other insects nestled in the leaves. To bring them out, soak freshly cut artichokes in salted ice water at least 30 minutes. Rinse the artichokes, and with a sharp knife cut the stems flush with the bottom. Then cut off the top quarter of the artichoke and snip off remaining leaf tips halfway down. To avoid discoloration, immediately place in water to which lemon juice or vinegar has been added. If desired, scrape out the choke before cooking and tie back together.

For the best flavor, cook the artichokes in stock to cover (lamb is especially good) flavored with onion, garlic and oregano sautéed together in olive oil. They are also good steamed or baked with herbs and olive oil, or cut into eighths, removing chokes, and stir fried in butter. Regardless of the method used, lemon juice should always be added when cooking.

Serve artichokes hot with hollandaise or béarnaise sauce, flavored or burnt butter, or lemon juice. Serve cold with mayonnaise, sour cream, egg or vinaigrette sauce. Stuff cold whole artichokes with crab and/or prawn salad, hot with scrambled eggs or creamed fish.

Add cooked artichoke hearts, whole or cut up, to casseroles, omelettes and frittatas. Serve cold cooked hearts stuffed with liver pâté or egg salad spread; or hot ones stuffed with spinach soufflé, sautéed mushrooms or a poached egg.

The leaves of the artichoke plant itself are edible. Though bitter, they perhaps are worth some experimentation in the kitchen.

Artichoke

ARTICHOKE APPETIZER PUFFS

Thaw in refrigerator overnight:
about 12 ounces
frozen puff pastry
Combine:
12 ounces cream cheese, softened
2 tablespoons butter, softened
2 eggs, beaten
4 tablespoons finely chopped
chives
1 teaspoon each grated onion
and Worcestershire sauce
6 drops Tabasco
10 to 12 ounces very finely
chopped cooked artichoke
bottoms
1/2 teaspoon salt
1/4 teaspoon freshly ground
white pepper
Adjust seasonings to taste and
chill. Roll puff pasty 1/16
inch thick and cut into 36 2-1/4-
inch rounds. Press into 36 tiny
patty pans (save scraps for other
use) and fill with artichoke
mixture. Sprinkle with:
paprika
Chill 30 minutes, then bake in
400° oven 12 minutes, or until
bubbly and slightly browned.
Makes 36 puffs

ARTICHOKE SCRAMBLE

Trim as directed:
6 medium large or 24 small
artichokes
Cut large ones into eighths,
small ones into halves, remove
chokes and set aside in water to
which has been added:
vinegar or lemon juice
Sauté in:
3 tablespoons butter
1 pound trimmed and thinly
sliced chicken gizzards
When slightly browned push aside
and sauté until transparent:
1 small onion, finely chopped
1 teaspoon finely chopped garlic

Drain and dry artichokes, add
to pan and brown slightly.
Then add:
8 ounces chopped, peeled and
seeded tomatoes
4 tablespoons finely chopped
parsley
1 tablespoon tomato paste
1 teaspoon salt
1/2 teaspoon each oregano and
paprika
1/4 teaspoon freshly ground
black pepper
Cover and cook, stirring often,
until artichokes are tender,
adding if needed:
tomato juice and/or stock
Adjust seasonings. Add:
10 eggs, beaten
3 to 6 ounces fresh bean sprouts,
crisped in ice water and
drained
Cook until partially set, toss with
fork and continue cooking until
eggs are done to taste. Serve on
halved, toasted rolls and
garnish with:
lemon wedges
finely chopped chives
Serves 8 to 10

ARTICHOKE AND SWEETBREAD PIE

To Make Pastry:
Combine:
2-1/2 ounces grated medium-sharp Cheddar cheese
4-1/2 ounces unbleached flour
1/2 teaspoon each salt and dry mustard
4 tablespoons finely chopped parsley
With fork, stir in to make dough that holds together:
5 to 6 tablespoons melted butter
Press into bottom and sides of 9-inch pie dish, cover and chill 30 minutes (or freeze up to 1 week). Before filling, prick shell in several places with fork and bake at 475° for 10 minutes.

To Make Filling:
Sauté 5 minutes, covered, in:
3 tablespoons butter
4 ounces thinly sliced onions
1 large stalk celery, diagonally sliced
2 tablespoons finely chopped celery leaves
Sprinkle with:
2 tablespoons flour

Cook and stir 3 minutes and then gradually add:
6 fluid ounces each liquid in which sweetbreads were cooked and creamy milk
1/2 teaspoon salt
1/4 teaspoon freshly ground white pepper
Cook and stir until thickened. Remove from heat and beat a small amount into:
2 eggs, beaten
Return eggs to rest of mixture and add:
6 to 8 ounces sliced cooked sweet-breads (page 178)
9 to 12 ounces sliced, cooked artichoke bottoms
Adjust seasonings and cool. Fill pastry shell with mixture and sprinkle with:
paprika
Bake in 400° oven 15 minutes. Lower heat to 325° and bake 15 minutes, or until toothpick inserted in center comes out clean. Let cool slightly before cutting into wedges. Serve with tomato-lettuce salad.
Serves 6 to 8

Asparagus

(Asparagus officinalis)

Cultivated for hundreds of years for its edible shoots, asparagus was originally considered only of medicinal value—to prevent bee stings and to relieve heart trouble. It first grew wild on the salt steppes of Eastern Europe before the Greeks and Romans began gathering its seeds for garden cultivation and gave it its name. Dried stalks were sometimes quickly boiled, though the crisp succulence of freshly cooked shoots probably had more to do with the wide acceptance of asparagus in England and elsewhere 350 years ago.

Left to grow to maturity, asparagus becomes a decorative plant with red berries. The best of both worlds can be enjoyed by cutting and cooking most of the shoots, yet leaving a few to mature. Male plants tend to produce many more shoots than the female, which produce berries, so one must strike a compromise between more eating (by removing berried plants) and viewing (by letting nature take its course).

Asparagus can be established by buying plants or by planting your own seed in April one inch deep in rows one foot apart, thinning later to one foot spacing. In either case, adequate bed preparation is well worth some extra effort. The best type of soil is a good deep loam

ASPARAGUS
Asparagus officinalis
Herbaceous perennial
4 to 6 feet in height
Fast grower
Propagate from seed
Sun
Hardy except in coldest areas
Young shoots eaten
Harvest shoots in March,
2 seasons after planting
White flowers, red berries

with a high humus content. If the soil is on the light side, compost and humus must be added. As asparagus remains in the same bed for many years, it is a good idea to double dig the ground. This means removing the first spit, forming a trench, forking over the bottom of the trench and adding compost or other humus. Then the top spit of the next layer is placed on the bottom of the trench and the bottom is forked over, adding compost or humus again. This operation should be repeated until the bed has been prepared. Beds should be four feet wide. Three rows of plants 15 inches apart is ideal for production.

When planting crowns of purchased plants or thinned-out seed plantings, dig a hole approximately 10 inches deep and make a four- to five-inch mound of compost on the bottom. Place the plant on the mound, cover the roots with fine soil and then fill the hole. The crown of the plant should be no more than four to five inches deep when finished. Shallower initial planting in troughs and gradual filling in will prevent plants being "suffocated" as they establish themselves. If blanched or white asparagus is desired, mound the soil around the shoots as they grow.

Harvesting of shoots by cutting four inches below the surface is not advisable until the third year. Top dress each winter with well-rotted manure.

Even if decorative mature plants are not a primary object, it is desirable to let a few shoots flower to maintain healthy growth. These shoots, as well as the stalks of developing plants, should be cut back to ground level at the end of the growing season.

Asparagus spears are best if picked as soon as they appear in the spring. In the summer, the beautiful fronds of the plant may be used in floral arrangements to brighten a kitchen.

Scrub the spears well with a vegetable brush and snap the lower part of the stalks off where they break readily. Save the ends for soup. Tie the spears in bundles and steam in the bottom of a double boiler or in a coffee pot, saving the cooking water for soup or for cooking potatoes. Asparagus may also be sliced on the diagonal and stir fried in a wok or heavy pan in butter and/or corn oil, adding a slice of ginger, a garlic clove and sesame or poppy seeds if desired. Cook asparagus only until tender; overcooking will destroy the flavor and texture.

ASPARAGUS PURÉE

Cut 4- to 5-inch spears from:
2-1/2 pounds asparagus
Place spears in plastic bag and refrigerate. Cut up stems and combine with:
4 ounces shredded Webbs lettuce
4 onion slices
1 bay leaf
4 thyme or lemon thyme sprigs
1 garlic clove
3/4 pint milk
1/2 teaspoon salt
1/4 teaspoon freshly ground white pepper
Bring to gentle boil, cover and simmer 20 minutes. Discard bay leaf, thyme and tough asparagus stems. Strain, reserving milk, and purée in blender, sieving if necessary to make smooth purée. Heat until bubbly:
1 tablespoon butter
Sprinkle with:
1 tablespoon flour
Cook and stir 3 minutes and then gradually add:
1/2 pint reserved milk (save rest to add to mashed potatoes)
reserved purée
Cook and stir until thickened. Continue cooking, stirring often, 10 minutes. Cool and jar.
May be frozen; defrost and reheat before using.

Asparagus

ASPARAGUS CREAM CHEESE SPREAD

Combine:
4 ounces cream cheese, softened
scant 1/4 pint asparagus purée (preceding)
1/2 teaspoon dry mustard
salt and freshly ground white pepper to taste
Blend in:
3 ounces finely chopped smoked ham, flaked crab meat or chopped prawns
Chill, mound on serving platter and garnish with:
tiny asparagus tips cooked just tender in salted water
Sprinkle with:
paprika
Serve with bland crackers or melba rounds.
Or to serve as a canapé, spread on toast cutouts, sprinkle with paprika and garnish with a tiny asparagus spear.
Makes approximately 30 cracker servings or canapés

ASPARAGUS POACHED-EGG CASSEROLE

Cut into small julienne strips:
1/2 cucumber, peeled
Sprinkle with salt, let stand 20 minutes, drain and dry.
Set aside.
Lightly poach:
6 eggs
Immediately cool in ice water to stop cooking, drain and trim whites. Chop trimmings and reserve. Heat:
1-1/4 pints asparagus purée (preceding)
1/4 pint creamy milk
Gradually beat 6 to 8 tablespoons of mixture into:
1 beaten egg

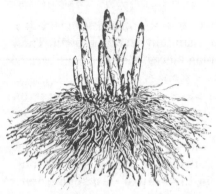

Return to rest of sauce and add:
1 to 2 teaspoons lemon or lime juice
Keep warm.
Steam in salted water until just tender:
asparagus spears from purée recipe
Add to sauce:
reserved chopped egg trimmings
reserved cucumber
Reheat without boiling, adjust seasonings and cover bottom of shallow baking dish with one-third of sauce. Arrange on top:
6 pieces buttered toast
Top each piece with:
poached egg
Arrange asparagus on top and around eggs and cover with remaining sauce. Sprinkle with:
6 tablespoons grated mild Cheddar cheese
paprika
Bake in 400° oven until heated through and bubbly. Serve with:
generous sprinkling of finely chopped parsley
Serves 6

ASPARAGUS CASSEROLE

Cut 5-inch spears from:
2-1/2 to 3 pounds asparagus
Reserve stems for soup or other use. Place spears in steamer with:
3/4 pint water
4 large onion slices
1/2 bay leaf
3 sprigs lemon thyme
1 garlic clove (optional)
1/2 teaspoon salt
1/4 teaspoon white pepper
Bring to boil and steam spears 5 minutes or until just tender. Remove spears and cool in ice water; drain and reserve. Reduce cooking water by half, strain and measure. There should be 1/2 pint. Melt until bubbly:
2 tablespoons butter
Sprinkle with:
2 tablespoons flour
Cook and stir 3 minutes and then gradually add:
reserved cooking water
1/4 pint double cream
Cook and stir until thickened. Season with:
1/8 teaspoon nutmeg
salt and white pepper to taste

Divide asparagus into 6 bundles and wrap each in:
4 or 5 slices prosciutto, or
1 thin slice ham
Cover bottom of shallow baking dish with one-third of the sauce. Arrange wrapped spears on top and pour rest of sauce over. Sprinkle with:
6 to 8 tablespoons grated Parmesan
paprika
Bake in 400° oven until heated through and bubbly.
Serves 6

SERVING HINTS

Mix cooked spears with:
• Sautéed mushrooms and sliced water chestnuts.
• Cooked peas or pea pods; dress with butter.

Dress cooked spears with:
• Melted butter and/or lime juice and buttered toasted almonds.
• Curried cream sauce.
• Hollandaise sauce made with lemon, orange or lime juice, or combination.
• Lobster, prawn or crab cream sauce, made with brandy; heat in a buttered casserole.
• Chopped hard-boiled egg, bread crumbs, parsley and lemon juice.

Toss cooked spears with:
• Grated Gruyère cheese and pine nuts.
• Melted butter, chopped hard-boiled egg.
• Salted cashews, butter, oregano and lemon juice.
• Finely chopped shallots, chopped parsley and melted butter.
• Garlic salt, lemon juice and nutmeg; sprinkle with grated Parmesan cheese and paprika.
• Melted butter and sesame seeds.
• Melted butter, bread crumbs, finely chopped celery and onion, lemon juice and a small amount of crumbled blue cheese.

In vinaigrette sauce, marinate young spears that have been cooked until just tender and use as a garnish for a raw mushroom and crab salad. Or marinate, drain and dry the spears and combine with prawns in an aspic salad. or wrap in prosciutto and serve as an appetizer. Young tender spears may be served raw with other vegetables and a dipping sauce.

Bay

(Laurus nobilis)

BAY
Laurus nobilis
Evergreen aromatic tree
30 to 60 feet in height
Fast grower
Propagate from seed or cuttings
Sun or light shade
Hardy
Leaves eaten
Harvest year round

The laurel or bay tree has a history that spans mythology, medicine and the arts.

When Apollo chided Cupid for his conduct, Cupid retaliated with two arrows, the first to make Apollo fall in love with the first female he encountered, the second to make him unappealing. Apollo met Daphne. He was enamored; she was repelled. While fleeing, she pleaded for escape. Athene obliged by changing her into the laurel tree (which the Greeks called "Daphne"), whose leaves Apollo, saddened but still loving, then proclaimed should crown the heads of all victors.

The word *baccalaureate* (laurel berry) is derived from the tradition of placing laurel leaves under a poet's pillow, and if his works were read in the university, he was crowned with the leaves and berries. This custom survived in Renaissance Europe where a distinguished poet or scholar of the universities of Oxford and Cambridge was crowned with a laurel wreath, also giving rise to the English term poet laureate. The word bachelor, from the same derivation, described the student who kept his head in his books and had no time to be concerned with matrimony.

The bay leaf's clean pungency assumed powers as an averter of ill: to ward off lightning and wizards, to safeguard dispatches from generals to emperors and to cleanse the air of pestilence. Even today bay leaves are prized as protection against weevils when scattered in cupboards and in amongst flour, crackers and spices.

The *Laurus nobilis,* the true laurel or bay tree, is native to the Mediterranean region and forms a small tree up to about 30 feet in height. It is hardy in many parts of Britain, easy to grow (propagated from seeds if desired) and is not demanding as to soil conditions.

Long used in the kitchen, the wholesome, aromatic leaves of the bay tree add a delightful pungency to many foods. Boughs of fresh bay leaves may also be added to all kinds of floral arrangements for beauty, fragrance and body. The dried bay leaf releases an intense flavor so that its addition must be done with a cautious, experienced hand. Commonly an ingredient for a bouquet garni for roasting chicken or other fowl, bay also complements the flavor of fish, venison and beef kidney. Bay is used in the preparation of corned beef and sauerbraten and many smoked meats. Add bay leaves to soups, tomato-based spaghetti sauces, meat marinades, vegetable cocktails and to the cooking water when boiling vegetables. For a different drink, enjoy an essence of bay in a martini or in a glass of 7-Up.

Fresh bay leaves may also be used as a flavoring. Skewer for barbecuing fresh-picked leaves and fish chunks; marinate pork in white wine, onion chunks stuck with cloves, peppercorns, garlic and bay and cook over hot coals. In the recipes that follow, fresh bay may be substituted for dry, but it must be remembered that since the flavor is not so intense the amount must be increased. Unlike most fresh leaves, bay does not soften after cooking; always remove leaves before serving.

TOMATO SAUCE

Sauté until salt pork is starting to brown:

1 tablespoon butter

2 tablespoons finely diced salt pork or fat bacon

Sprinkle with:

2 tablespoons flour

1/2 teaspoon sugar

Stir and add:

6 tablespoons each diced onion, carrot and celery with some leaves

Cook and stir until slightly browned. Then add:

12 ripe tomatoes (about 2 pounds), peeled and chopped, or

1 28-ounce can tomatoes, drained

2 large sprigs parsley

2 thyme sprigs

2 dried bay leaves

1/4 pint concentrated chicken stock

Blend well and, stirring occasionally, cook 1-1/2 hours on medium heat, covered. Remove thyme sprigs and bay leaves and purée mixture in blender. Return to saucepan and season to taste with:

salt and pepper

Cook down or add water for desired consistency.

Makes approximately 1 pint

Bay

TURKEY CUTLETS

Pound between sheets of grease-proof paper until very thin:
2 turkey steaks (about 1-1/2 pounds)
Cut into 4 to 6 cutlets and marinate, turning often, for 3 hours in:
3 tablespoons lemon juice
6 to 8 tablespoons finely chopped spring onions
2 to 3 dried bay leaves, broken
Remove turkey from marinade and discard bay. Dry with paper towels (some onions can be left clinging to the meat).
Dip in:
beaten egg
Coat with:
seasoned flour
Refrigerate at least 1 hour. Sauté over medium heat to brown both sides in:
1 to 2 tablespoons each garlic olive oil and butter
Serve with tomato sauce flavored to taste with dry vermouth.
Serves 4

CALVES' LIVER AND AVOCADO

Turning often, marinate 3 to 4 hours in:
6 to 8 tablespoons sake or dry sherry
5 ounces finely chopped onions
2 or 3 dried bay leaves, halved
4 slices calves' liver
Remove liver, pat dry and sprinkle lightly with:
flour
salt
white pepper
Strain onions and discard bay leaves. Sauté covered until soft in:
2 tablespoons butter
the finely chopped onions
Push aside and, adding more butter if needed, sauté liver slices, turning once, until browned and cooked to taste. Do not overcook or liver will toughen. It should be slightly pink inside. Remove liver and onions to heated platter and keep warm. Sauté 1 minute per side, adding more butter if needed:
1 large avocado, peeled and sliced
Arrange avocado slices around liver and onions and to sauté pan add:

1 tablespoon butter
1-1/2 tablespoons lemon juice
6 to 8 tablespoons finely chopped parsley
4 tablespoons rich beef stock
Heat quickly and pour over liver, onions and avocado.
Sprinkle lightly with:
paprika
Serve immediately.
Serves 4

CHICKEN GIZZARD RUMAKI
(Appetizers)

Place in saucepan:
1 pound chicken gizzards
1 onion, sliced
2 parsley sprigs
1 thyme sprig
2 dried bay leaves
Add just enough boiling water to cover. Bring back to boil, cover and simmer until gizzards are tender. Strain and reserve liquid to add to soup stock. Trim fat and gristle from gizzards and cut in halves or quarters. Wrap each piece in:
bacon cooked just to soften
Skewer and grill until bacon is crisp.
Makes approximately 30 rumaki

Scarlet Runner Bean

(Phaseolus coccineus and cultivars)

In its native habitat of South America the scarlet runner bean was always valued as a perennial producer of high-protein, easily stored beans. But when first introduced into Europe in 1633 it was regarded only as an ornamental. This handsome climber immediately found favor for its ability to climb any pole or support quickly and to foliate profusely.

A member of the leguminous family, the scarlet runner bean is ideal for the garden as it leaves the soil richer in nitrogen than when it is planted. This is because of the bacteria which live in the root nodules in a symbiotic relationship with the plant. This legume bacteria takes the "free" nitrogen of the air, "fixes" it and returns it to the soil, thus enriching the soil with nutrients the plant can use.

The stems can be lifted and stored over the winter in a dry frostproof area for replanting in the spring, but planting the beans themselves is easier. Pick a sunny site with ground well forked over with compost or other humus. After frost danger has passed, firm the ground well, drill five-inch deep holes, and drop in four or five seeds. Later thin the shoots to the strongest stalk around which soil should be moulded to anchor the plant securely.

The scarlet runner likes lots of water when growing, and a fine spray in the late evening and early morning over the foliage and brilliant-red flowers helps the fruit to set. Keep growing area clean and weed free to prevent rust and chocolate spot. Though they are infrequent visitors, also watch for aphid invasion.

The pods of the scarlet runner bean should be picked when young and green, about six to eight inches in length. Wash well, snip off the top and tail and pull out the string along one side. These beans should not be cooked whole, but rather sliced across or on the narrow diagonal. Cook rapidly in boiling unsalted water, adding dried or fresh savory to taste. Drain immediately, saving cooking water for soup stock, and add seasonings. More mature pods can be picked and shelled, and cooked as you would broad beans.

SCARLET RUNNER BEAN
Phaseolus coccineus *and cultivars*
Perennial; treat as annual
in colder areas
Climber to 8 to 9 feet in height
Fast grower
Propagate from seed
Sun
Not hardy
Pods eaten
Flowers in spring
Harvest in summer
Scarlet flowers, green bean pods

Scarlet Runner Bean

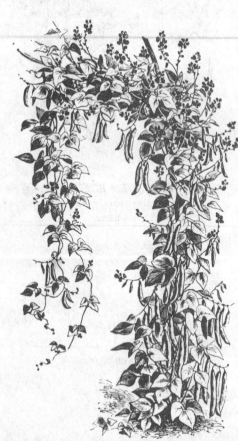

SERVING HINTS

Toss cooked beans with:
- Butter, sautéed mushrooms, sour cream and finely chopped parsley or basil.
- Butter, sliced water chestnuts, soy sauce and lemon juice.
- Cooked peas, carrots, celery and/or corn, chopped pimiento and butter.
- Butter, sautéed onions, finely chopped parsley and a little vinegar.
- Sautéed onions and sour cream; sprinkle with crisp-cooked bacon bits.
- Butter, anchovy paste and finely chopped parsley.
- Crumbs sautéed in butter with garlic.
- Butter, finely chopped parsley and lemon juice.
- Butter, beef stock, soy sauce and lime juice.
- Butter, slivered toasted almonds and chopped dill.

Dress cooked beans with:
- Parsley sauce (page 129) made with water in which beans were cooked.
- Fresh tomato sauce with mushrooms.

Sliced runner beans may also be stir fried in corn oil with garlic and ginger, or butter steamed until tender. These beans are especially good served with fish such as sole amandine or baked salmon.

BEANS WITH COCONUT

Bring to boil:
1-1/4 pints water
2 slices ginger root
1 large garlic clove
6 coriander seeds, lightly crushed
1/8 teaspoon cayenne pepper
Simmer 10 minutes, bring back
to hard boil and add:
2 pounds beans, sliced
Bring back to boil and cook
quickly just until beans are
tender. Drain. Sauté until soft in:
4 tablespoons butter
4 ounces finely chopped onion
Combine with beans, season with
salt and pepper to taste and
transfer to heated serving dish.
Sprinkle with:
2 to 3 ounces finely grated
   unsweetened coconut
Serves 6

POTATO PATTIES
(Rissoles)

Combine, bring to boil and cook
until tender:
1 pound unpeeled white potatoes
water to cover
1/4 teaspoon salt
2 lavender cotton sprigs
6 parsley sprigs with stems
Drain, peel potatoes and mash.
Sauté until soft in:
1 tablespoon butter
1 small onion, finely chopped
3 tablespoons finely chopped garlic
   chive bulbs (page 62)
Add and brown lightly:
1/2 pound minced lean beef
Combine with potatoes and
blend in:
1/2 pound cooked sliced beans
2 eggs, beaten
salt and pepper to taste
Chill and form into 12 cakes.
Coat lightly with flour and brown
on both sides in:
2 tablespoons butter
Sprinkle with:
finely chopped parsley
grated Parmesan cheese
Serves 6

BEANS WITH FENNEL

Cook until just tender:
1-1/2 pounds runner beans, in
boiling water to cover
Drain (reserve water for soup)
and add to beans:
5 to 6 tablespoons butter,
   softened
3 to 4 ounces chopped tops of
   fennel with feathers
salt and freshly ground white
   pepper to taste
Reheat and serve immediately
sprinkled with:
finely chopped parsley
Serves 5 to 6

Birch

(Betula alba)

The birch is so familiar and ubiquitous no one seems to have bothered to record its history. Most famous for its unusual white or grey bark that can be peeled for making canoes and writing scrolls, or for making tannin to cure leather, the birch has through the ages also provided wood for many a cosy fire as well as for thread, mill bobbins, herring barrel staves, broom handles, charcoal, furniture and panelling. Wine from the sugary sap is drunk in some European countries, and young birch leaves can be made into a tea, or, in larger quantities, act as a mild laxative.

The birch's relaxed approach to growing makes it suitable for planting in almost any fairly dry soil, though it tolerates considerable water, too, if it must. Strong wind and sun don't seem to discourage it, and many a forest, street or garden has been adorned with its graceful beauty as a young tree or its majesty when full grown. Easily raised from a seed, the birch can also be rooted from hard-wood cuttings and is worthy of wider use in the garden.

The birch tree is well known as an ornamental, but little experimentation has been done with it in the kitchen. It produces tender young edible leaves in the early spring. These leaves are used for making tea and as greens by some North American Indians, and the buds and twigs are said to be "nibblers" for hikers, helping to allay thirst. The sawdust of the birchwood is used in the making of bread in Norway and Sweden; it is first boiled and baked and then mixed with flour. When harvesting the young leaves for eating, be careful to use only the smaller ones. Larger ones become bitter when cooked. The birch also produces catkins, tiny, drooping tassel-like spikes which contain the reproductive organs. These may be picked and eaten with the shoots and leaves if they are selected when very tiny, before they mature and brown.

46

STIR FRY PORK

Slice thinly on the diagonal:
1 pound lean pork shoulder
Combine with:
1 teaspoon cornflour
1/2 tablespoon soy sauce
1/2 teaspoon each salt and sugar
1 teaspoon sake or dry sherry
1 slice ginger root, chopped
1 garlic clove, chopped
In wok or heavy frying pan heat:
2 tablespoons corn oil
When oil begins to sizzle, add meat and cook quickly 2 minutes.
Add and cook rapidly 1 minute:
1/2 cup each sliced bamboo
shoots and water chestnuts
1 cup fresh pea pods
1/2 cup birch shoots
1 cup bean sprouts
Add and stir in:
4 to 6 tablespoons chicken stock
Cover and let steam 2 to 3 minutes until vegetables are just tender.
Serve over rice or freshly cooked fresh noodles.
Serves 4 to 6

BIRCH SHOOT SALAD

Wash, dry, wrap and chill:
4 ounces birch shoots
1 medium-size head
  lettuce, torn in pieces
To make dressing, combine:
2-1/2 tablespoons red wine
  vinegar
6–8 tablespoons walnut salad oil
1 tablespoon German-style
  mustard
2 tablespoons finely chopped parsley
salt and freshly ground pepper
  to taste
finely chopped garlic to taste
  (optional)
Just before serving, combine
greens in a bowl and toss with
dressing. Sprinkle on top of salad:
sieved hard-boiled egg
Serves 6

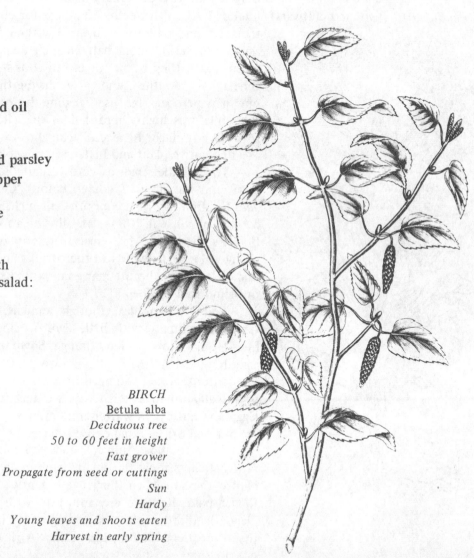

BIRCH
Betula alba
Deciduous tree
50 to 60 feet in height
Fast grower
Propagate from seed or cuttings
Sun
Hardy
Young leaves and shoots eaten
Harvest in early spring

Calendula

(Calendula officinalis and cultivars)

Related to the chrysanthemum, daisy and dandelion, the calendula or marigold, as it is commonly called, is native to Southern Europe. Mawes' dictionary from the 18th century specifies, "While intended to cultivate the first sort for culinary uses, may either sow the seeds and rake them in, or sow them in small shallow drills a foot asunder covering them half an inch deep. Their flowers being their useful parts, they be fit for use in consistent succession from time to time in dry weather, and, after drying them in the shade, should be put in paper bags for use." From this quote it can be seen that the calendula was highly regarded in the kitchen to the point of being sown like spinach. In recent years, however, it has been grown chiefly as a decorative plant and little used in cooking.

The Middle English word, "marigold," derives from the Virgin Mary and the flower's golden color. "Calendula" comes from *calendae,* the first day of the month on which interest was paid in its native habitat of ancient Rome, an allusion to its perpetual flowering. The flower's distinctive taste was formerly prized for making wine and giving color and flavor to other drinks and a variety of dishes. It was said that those who ate marigolds would see fairies, be more amorous, or be induced to sleep.

Today calendulas, though annuals, give color all summer in temperate climate with little care—in singles, doubles and in various hues from yellow to deep orange. Sown in half-inch drills in ordinary, well-drained soil from March into May, calendulas can be thinned out or transplanted and need little water. They like full sun and flower prolifically up to a height of two feet, then have a tendency to get leggy and untidy. In wetter areas mildew may attack unless side shoots are pinched off to avoid dense foliage.

As with most flower petals, calendulas add color and texture rather than strong flavor to drinks and foods. Gather the flowers before the sun is on them, wash gently and pull the petals from the flower base. Remove any moisture with paper towels and place in a plastic bag in the refrigerator until ready to use. Be careful to use only the true calendula for eating; the "African marigold" or "tagetes" is not suitable.

SERVING HINTS

- If using as a garnish for meat dishes, canapés, cream soups, chowders, stuffed eggs and the like, crisp the petals in ice water.
- Add chopped petals to mashed potatoes or turnips, dumplings and salads.
- Combine equal amounts prawn or lobster bisque and cream cheese, season to taste with lemon juice and chopped chives and petals; serve on cooked cauliflower, beans or asparagus.
- Scramble eggs with bits of cream cheese and just before the eggs are set add chopped petals and parsley.
- Stir fry cauliflowerets in a wok with a slice of ginger root, several whole cloves and a small stick of cinnamon. When cooked, sprinkle with grated orange peel and chopped petals.
- Add chopped petals to chicken liver pâté and sprinkle with toasted sesame seeds.
- Season stuffed eggs with chopped petals or crumbled dried petals.

DRIED PETALS

For a more concentrated flavor, the petals can be dried as directed on page 27. Crumble the dried petals and add to sauces, cream cheese, cakes, chicken pie, mashed potatoes, bread puddings and rice or noodle dishes for color and subtle flavor.

CALENDULA
Calendula officinalis
and cultivars
Annual, suitable for bedding
18 inches in height
Fast grower
Propagate from seed
Sun
Hardy
Flowers eaten
Sow in spring; successive sowings create continual flowering in warm areas
Orange flowers; sometimes double

Calendula

CALENDULA EGG SPREAD

Combine:
5 tablespoons home-made mayonnaise
1 tablespoon finely chopped
onion
6 to 8 tablespoons finely chopped
celery
1/2 teaspoon curry powder or to
taste
1/4 teaspoon dry mustard
3 drops Tabasco
salt and freshly ground
white pepper to taste
Fold in:
4 hard-boiled eggs, chopped
4 tablespoons finely chopped
calendula petals
Place in serving bowl, cover and
refrigerate. Just before serving
sprinkle with:
paprika
Serve with bland crackers or
rye bread.
Also good as filling for artichoke
bottoms, baked pastry shells or
for stuffing small tomatoes
Makes a generous 1/4 pint.

CALENDULA RAMEKIN

Combine:
12 ounces diced cooked chicken
or turkey
3 to 4 stalks celery, finely chopped
4 tablespoons finely chopped
green pepper
3 tablespoons grated onion
2 tablespoons each finely chopped
chives and parsley
2 tablespoons lemon juice
1/2 teaspoon salt
1/4 teaspoon each garlic powder,
paprika, pepper and poultry
seasoning
1/2 pint mayonnaise
6 to 8 tablespoons chopped
calendula petals
Divide between 4 to 6 buttered
ramekins and sprinkle with
mixture of:
**about 2 ounces buttered bread
crumbs**
**1 ounce grated sharp Cheddar
cheese**
Bake in 450° oven 10 minutes or
until heated through and bubbly.
Garnish with:
parsley or watercress sprigs
Serves 4 to 6

COLD CREAM CHEESE SOUP

Cut into pieces and place in
blender:
8 ounces cream cheese, softened
Add to blender:
1 10-1/2-ounce can chicken
consommé
1/2 teaspoon curry powder
1 garlic clove, finely chopped
1/2 teaspoon grated lemon peel
Purée until smooth and refrigerate
at least 4 hours. Adjust seasonings with:
freshly ground white pepper
curry powder
Serve in chilled bowls with
garnish of:
dab of lumpfish caviar
Sprinkle with:
finely chopped parsley
chopped calendula petals
Serves 4

CHAMOMILE
Anthemis nobilis
Perennial ground cover
To 6 inches in height
Fast grower
Propagate by division or cuttings
Sun or light shade
Hardy except in coldest areas
Flowers and leaves eaten
Harvest in late spring and summer
Yellow flowers

Chamomile

(Anthemis nobilis)

Throughout history, chamomile has been highly regarded for its medicinal properties and its beautiful fragrance. Its name comes from the Greek, *chamai* meaning earth and *melon* meaning apple; in Spanish it is called *manzanilla,* "little apple." Yet this plant bears no fleshy fruit similar to the apple. It is rather its tiny, fragrant apple-shaped flowers that have been so prized.

Chamomile

The Egyptians believed chamomile cured the ague. During the Middle Ages it was one of the herbs strewn on floors, so its beautiful fragrance would be released when trod upon. Parkinson in 1629 in his *Earthly Paradise* wrote: "Camomil is put to divers and sundry uses both for pleasure and profit, both for the sick and the sound, in bathing to comfort and strengthen the sound and to ease the pains in the diseased." An infusion of one ounce of dried flowers to 3/4 pint of water is said to have a grand, soothing effect and is absolutely harmless. As the "plant's physician," chamomile was grown close to sick or droopy plants to help them recover.

In the garden, the yellow and grey-green chamomile makes an ideal perennial ground cover for a dry area with little foot traffic, forming a creeping mat and, from time to time, small hummocks. While it can be raised from seed, propagation by lifting and separating older plants and replanting six inches apart in the spring (four inches if light traffic is expected) is better. Keep free of weeds until bed is established and remove dead flowers that have not been harvested. Older plants tend to die out, but this can be remedied by lifting and replanting the younger ones. There are few pests to worry about, and while sun is preferred, the chamomile will do well in partial shade.

The tiny, deep yellow flowers of the chamomile plant have long been used dried for making tea. Flavored with honey and a little grated orange rind, the tea has a distinctive, unusual taste. In the past, syrup and beer were made, and brandy was infused with the dried flowers. Snip flowers off with scissors, being sure to use only those in full bloom. Once they have started to darken, they lose their flavor. Wash and pat dry thoroughly, place on a rack or mesh screen and let dry in a warm place.

Although the leaves do not have a history of culinary use, the small sprigs can be treated as a seasoning, in the manner of bay leaf, to lend a subtle flavor to cream sauces, butter, honey and sour cream. Chamomile butter and sour cream are excellent on baked potatoes with a sprinkling of chopped parsley. The chamomile honey can be used in any recipe calling for honey. Gather sprigs of medium age. The tiny ones do not have enough flavor; the large ones are too strong.

TURKEY RICE CASSEROLE

For the sauce, melt until bubbly:
5 tablespoons butter
Add:
4 tablespoons flour
1/2 teaspoon salt
1/4 teaspoon freshly ground
    white pepper
1/8 teaspoon freshly grated
    nutmeg
4 or 5 chamomile sprigs
Cook and stir without browning
3 minutes. Gradually add:
1 pint creamy milk
Cook and stir until smooth and
thickened; continue cooking,
stirring often, 10 minutes.
Remove from heat, discard
chamomile and swirl in to prevent crust from forming:
1 teaspoon softened butter
Set aside.
Sauté, covered, 5 minutes in:
4 tablespoons butter
4 ounces diced mushrooms
6 to 8 tablespoons each finely
    chopped celery with some
    leaves, green pepper and onion
Add to sauce with:
12 ounces cubed cooked turkey
Cook and stir over medium heat
10 minutes, adding if too thick:
creamy milk

Remove from heat and add:
1 2-ounce jar sweet red peppers,
    chopped
3 tablespoons Madeira (optional)
Set aside.
Place in bottom of heavily
buttered shallow casserole:
1 pound rice, freshly cooked
Sprinkle with:
1/4 teaspoon celery salt
1/8 teaspoon freshly ground
    black pepper
Pour turkey mixture over rice
and sprinkle with:
paprika
Bake in 350° oven 30 minutes or
until heated through. If making
ahead and refrigerating, cook
40 minutes or longer.
Serves 4 to 6

SCALLOP RAMEKINS

Combine and simmer 10
minutes:
1/2 pint white wine
1/4 pint fish stock
1 onion, sliced
2 parsley sprigs
4 chamomile sprigs
4 peppercorns, lightly crushed
1/2 teaspoon salt
Bring to fast boil and add:
2 pounds scallops, halved if large

Lower heat and simmer 5 minutes. Strain and reserve liquid.
Slice scallops and set aside.
Sauté in:
2 ounces butter
1/2 pound mushrooms, sliced
Add and cook 10 minutes,
stirring often:
4 large ripe tomatoes, peeled,
    seeded and chopped (if using
    canned, drain)
4 to 6 chamomile sprigs
Remove from heat, discard chamomile and add scallops. Melt:
2 tablespoons butter
Sprinkle with:
2 tablespoons flour
Gradually add, cooking and
stirring until thickened:
1/2 pint reserved liquid
Combine with scallops and divide
between 6 ramekins or scallop
shells. Sprinkle with:
bread crumbs
Dot with:
butter
Bake in 400° oven until heated
and bubbly. Sprinkle with:
finely chopped parsley
paprika
Serves 6

SPANISH CHESTNUT
Castanea sativa
Deciduous tree
To 100 feet in height
Rate of growth varies
Propagate from cuttings or seed
Sun
Hardy
Nuts eaten
Flowers in summer
Harvest in autumn
Tree bears when 10 to 12
years old
Yellow catkins, brown nuts

Spanish Chestnut

(Castanea sativa)

A member of the *Fagaceae* (beech) family, which includes not only the chestnut but also the beech, oak and numerous shrubs, the *C. sativa* originated around the Mediterranean and was first recorded about 500 B.C. It is preferred for ornamental use to the smaller American native, *C. dentata*, which is said to have a sweeter nut and better timber. *C. sativa* is a tall-growing, though not wide-spreading tree that reaches a tremendous girth in Britain, one of the many countries where the Romans introduced it on their colonizing travels. It is most at home in sun-drenched, dry places spurned by most other trees.

Chestnut wood, most durable taken from young trees, is ideal for making wine casks: it imparts no unpleasant taste and holds evaporation to a minimum. The nuts have long provided a variety of dishes in southern France and Italy: flour for elaborate breads, cakes and porridges; a direct substitute for bread or potatoes when roasted.

Chestnut trees can easily be grown from ripe nuts in lime-free soil. Plant in early autumn three inches deep in good soil with proper drainage. During the next summer they will grow several feet, after which they can be lifted and planted in final positions. Young container-grown trees require especially well-prepared soil. When young, prune trees to shape; later, thin out branches to obtain a well-balanced tree. Little special care is needed for established trees. A number of varieties are available with variegated and various shades of leaves. The pyramidal form is especially suited to smaller gardens.

Chestnuts are ready to eat when they start falling from the tree. While it may seem troublesome to separate the nuts from their spiny seed coverings, their delicious flavor makes it worthwhile. Chestnuts are used raw or cooked in a variety of ways. If using raw, simply peel with a sharp knife. If planning to boil, steam or grill them, make an X on the flat side of each chestnut. Working with a dozen or so at a time, place them in a saucepan, cover with water and boil until the skins can be peeled off with a sharp knife. Be sure to peel them while they are still hot or the inner brown fur-like skin, which must be removed, will not come off easily.

Roast unpeeled chestnuts without prior boiling and let your guests peel their own. Whole peeled chestnuts, wrapped in bacon and grilled, can be served with scrambled eggs for breakfast or brunch. For a dessert, steep whole chestnuts in heavy syrup.

Finely chopped or puréed, chestnuts can be used hot in stuffings, nutmeg-seasoned cream sauce and croquettes. Use cold in soufflés, ices, puddings, confectioneries, as a kirsch-flavored filling for barquettes and in sweetened cream and brandy.

Spanish Chestnut

CHESTNUT PURÉE

Combine:
1 pound chestnuts, peeled and
   chopped
3 celery stalks and leaves, cut
   in large pieces
1 medium-size onion, quartered
6 or 8 whole nutmeg geranium
   leaves
5 tablespoons water
1 tablespoon cider vinegar
1/4 teaspoon salt
1/8 teaspoon freshly ground
   white pepper
Cover, bring to gentle boil, and
simmer 20 minutes or until chestnuts are tender, adding water as
needed. Discard celery, onion
and geranium leaves. Add:
2 to 3 tablespoons butter
4 to 6 tablespoons double cream
Purée in blender, reheat and
adjust seasonings. If too
thick, thin with:
more cream
Sprinkle with:
finely chopped parsley
Serve as accompaniment to
venison or other game. Or fill
heated artichoke bottoms and
serve as garnish for any meat
or poultry dish.
Makes a scant 3/4 pint

CHESTNUT CREAM-CHEESE SPREAD

Cream:
5 ounces cream cheese, softened
2 to 3 teaspoons sour cream
Blend in:
1/2 pint chestnut purée (preceding)
2 tablespoons grated raw chestnut
salt and freshly ground white
   pepper to taste
dash cayenne pepper (optional)
Pack into crock and sprinkle with:
freshly grated raw chestnut
paprika
finely chopped parsley
Serve with bland crackers or
melba toast.
Makes a generous 1/2 pint

CHESTNUT EGG SPREAD

Mix together:
6 hard-boiled eggs, chopped
8 tablespoons chestnut purée
   (preceding)
4 tablespoons sour cream
2 tablespoons each finely chopped
   parsley and grated raw chestnut
Transfer to serving bowl and
sprinkle with:
paprika
finely chopped parsley
Serve with crackers or melba
rounds.

CHESTNUT-STUFFED EGGS

Peel and cut in half:
hard-boiled eggs
Mash yolks and for each egg add:
1 tablespoon chestnut purée
   (preceding) or to taste
sour cream or mild garlic French
   dressing
salt and freshly ground white
   pepper to taste
Stuff yolk mixture into white
halves and sprinkle with:
grated raw chestnut
paprika
Garnish each half with:
tiny parsley sprig

BAKED POTATOES
WITH CHESTNUTS

With apple corer hollow out
centers of:
6 baking potatoes
Save a "plug" for each end and
boil up remaining potato cores
for another use.
Stuff each potato with:
**2 tablespoons finely chopped
peeled chestnuts**
Replace "plugs" and partially
wrap potatoes in foil so that
chestnuts do not fall out. Bake
in 350° oven 1 hour or until
potatoes are soft. Open lengthwise and sprinkle with:
salt and pepper to taste
finely chopped parsley
Dot with:
softened butter
Serves 6

CHESTNUT SOUP

Combine:
**1/2 pound chestnuts, peeled
as directed**
1/2 pound red potatoes (unpeeled)
1-1/2 pints veal or chicken stock
**4 large stalks celery with leaves,
chopped**
6 tablespoons chopped mild onion
4 parsley sprigs
2 large thyme sprigs
1 large oregano sprig
1/2 teaspoon salt
**6 white peppercorns, lightly
crushed**
Cover, bring to gentle boil and
simmer 45 minutes or until
chestnuts are tender. Sieve, pushing as much pulp through as
possible. Return to saucepan
and reheat with:
about 1/2 pint creamy milk
Adjust seasonings and thin if
desired with:
stock
Just before serving swirl in:
**5 tablespoons butter, cut into
bits**
Sprinkle with:
finely chopped chives or parsley
Serves 6

CHESTNUT ICE
CREAM TOPPING

Combine:
**4 ounces finely chopped peeled
chestnuts**
4 to 6 tablespoons castor sugar
3 tablespoons rose water
2 thin slices orange peel
Cook, stirring often, until thick,
adding a little water if needed.
Chestnuts should remain crisp.
Discard orange peel and add:
1/4 teaspoon vanilla essence
Cool. Top scoops of vanilla ice
cream with 1 or 2 tablespoons
chestnut mixture and sprinkle
liberally with:
grated orange peel
Makes enough for approximately
8 servings

Chilean Guava

(Ugni molinae)

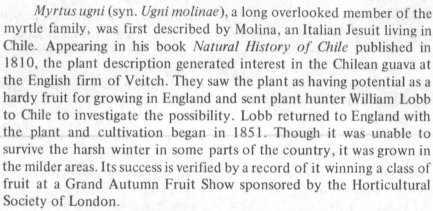

CHILEAN GUAVA
Myrtus ugni
Evergreen shrub
To 7 to 8 feet in height
Fast grower and spreader
Propagate from cuttings
Sun or light shade
Will not stand frost
Berries eaten
Flowers in summer
Harvest in autumn
White flowers, red berries

Myrtus ugni (syn. *Ugni molinae*), a long overlooked member of the myrtle family, was first described by Molina, an Italian Jesuit living in Chile. Appearing in his book *Natural History of Chile* published in 1810, the plant description generated interest in the Chilean guava at the English firm of Veitch. They saw the plant as having potential as a hardy fruit for growing in England and sent plant hunter William Lobb to Chile to investigate the possibility. Lobb returned to England with the plant and cultivation began in 1851. Though it was unable to survive the harsh winter in some parts of the country, it was grown in the milder areas. Its success is verified by a record of it winning a class of fruit at a Grand Autumn Fruit Show sponsored by the Horticultural Society of London.

The berries of the Chilean guava or *uñi,* as the Chileans call the plant, are the size of a garden pea. Brilliant red in color, they turn gradually darker as they ripen. Though commonly seen in the markets of Chile, their presence is rare in other parts of the world. In its native country, pies and jellies from this fruit are widely enjoyed. It is also recorded that Chilean guava jam was a favorite of Queen Victoria.

Semi-ripe wood cuttings taken in late summer and placed in a cold frame will root in a matter of weeks. One part each soil, sand and moss peat or leaf mould is best. If no cold frame is available, a tent of polythene, a foot high for ample ventilation and a foot square, can house 20 to 25 cuttings. Once they are rooted, transplant to separate four-inch pots for growing fuller roots and subsequent planting out in permanent locations.

Although the bright red berries of the Chilean guava somewhat resemble currants, their distinctive flavor is closer to that of strawberries. The berries are ripe when they easily separate from the bush; remove stem ends and wash. They may be eaten raw to add flavor and variety to mixed fruit salads and desserts, though the tiny seeds of this fruit may prove objectionable to some.

CHILEAN GUAVA SAUCE

Naturally sweet and full of pectin, the berries cook down into a beautiful deep reddish sauce, jelly or chutney. To make a sauce, cook berries with two-thirds as much water until soft. Sieve and add sugar to taste. Cook down to desired consistency and serve on vanilla ice cream, or as a topping for cheesecake or a fruit pie.

CHILEAN GUAVA JELLY

Bring to boil:
9 cups Chilean guava berries
6 cups water
Cover and cook over medium heat until berries are very soft. Wet a jelly bag and wring out well. Mash berries and transfer to bag. Hang bag over a saucepan or place on a strainer over saucepan. Let drip overnight to extract all juice. Discard pulp (or reuse for less concentrated batch of jelly) and bring liquid to boil. Skim any scum that rises to surface. Add:
2/3 cup sugar

Stir to dissolve sugar and boil rapidly 8 minutes. Start testing at this point by placing a small amount of syrup in a wooden spoon and cooling it slightly. Tip spoon and let syrup drop from side of spoon back into saucepan. As syrup thickens, 2 drops will form along the edge of the spoon on either side. When drops run together and drop as one, the firm jelly stage has been reached. Remove syrup from heat and pour immediately into hot sterilized jars to within 1/4 inch from the top. Seal. Store in dark, cool place. Spread on buttered toast or serve with any light meat or fowl.

COCKTAIL SAUSAGES WITH CHILEAN GUAVA JELLY

Combine in a saucepan and heat:
Chilean guava jelly
prepared mustard to taste
When well blended, add:
cooked cocktail sausages
Cover and cook over low heat 30 minutes. Serve in chafing dish with cocktail sticks.

POTATO CRÊPES

To make batter, in blender combine thoroughly:
1-1/2 cups milk, or
1 cup milk and 1/2 cup stock
2 eggs
1 cup unbleached flour
1/2 teaspoon salt
1/4 teaspoon sugar (optional)
1/4 teaspoon chopped lavender
Cover this batter and refrigerate at least 2 hours.
Wash (but do not peel), grate finely and add to batter:
1 pound white potatoes
In a 6- to 7-inch crêpe pan heat until bubbly:
1 teaspoon butter
Pour in about 4 tablespoons batter (stir often) and quickly tilt pan to cover bottom. Cook over medium heat until browned; then turn and brown other side. Remove and keep warm in a 350° oven. Adding butter as needed, continue with rest of batter.
Place on each crêpe:
2 teaspoons Chilean guava jelly
Fold and serve immediately as meat accompaniment.
Makes 12 crêpes

Chilean Guava

WILD BOAR CHOPS

Remove fat from:
8 wild boar chops*
Coat lightly with:
flour seasoned with salt, pepper and paprika
Brown on both sides in:
3 tablespoons oil and/or butter
Remove chops and sauté lightly, adding more oil and/or butter if needed:
1 large onion, sliced
Deglaze frying pan with:
3/4 pint pork stock (beef may be substituted, but is not as good)
Return chops to frying pan and sprinkle with:
1 tablespoon finely chopped sage
Cover tightly and cook over medium low heat 30 to 40 minutes depending upon thickness of chops, adding more stock if needed. Add to frying pan:
4 new white potatoes, unpeeled and thinly sliced
Cover and cook until potatoes are just tender. Transfer chops, potatoes and onions to heated serving platter. Add to juices and cook and stir to melt:
8 ounces Chilean guava jelly
stock if needed

Pour gravy over chops and serve with:
stir-fried courgettes or courgette pancakes (following recipe)
Serves 4

*If boar is old and gamey, marinate in mixture of:
dry red wine
juniper berries, lightly crushed
black peppercorns, slightly crushed
olive oil
Drain and dry before coating with flour.
The dish may also be prepared with 4 thick pork chops or venison steaks, marinated as above.

COURGETTE PANCAKES

Follow batter recipe for potato crêpes (page 59) substituting for the lavender:
1/2 teaspoon thyme
Add to batter:
3/4 pound courgettes, grated on medium-coarse grater
2 tablespoons finely chopped parsley
Cook as directed for potato crêpes.

SWEET AND SOUR CHICKEN

Combine:
2 tablespoons soy sauce
2 slices ginger root
4 tablespoons chopped chive or garlic chive bulbs (page 62)
1 tablespoon sake or dry sherry
Pour this mixture over:
1-1/2 pounds chicken meat, dark or light
Marinate at least 3 hours. Remove chicken from marinade and place in bowl. Mix in:
1 beaten egg
Sprinkle with:
5 tablespoons flour
Stir to coat pieces well and fry in hot oil 1/2 inch deep one layer at a time until golden on both sides. Drain and place on shredded lettuce.
Combine:
1/2 pint cold water
2 tablespoons each ketchup, vinegar, cornflour and sugar
2 to 3 tablespoons Chilean guava jelly or sauce
Heat until slightly thickened and adjust seasonings to taste. Pour over chicken and sprinkle with:
4 tablespoons toasted sesame seeds
Serve hot or lukewarm.
Serves 4 to 6

Chives

(Allium schoenoprasum)

The onion, leek and chive, bulb members of the lily family, are more noted for their distinctive taste and odor than their flowers. The chive's burst of purple or white blossoms in summer, though, is most attractive if the stalks have not been entirely consumed in all sorts of delicious ways. The scientific name of this branch of the lily family derives from the Latin *allium* meaning garlic, another famous member, though not as decorative as the chive.

Onions are native to the Mediterranean region and date back at least 2000 years in man's culinary history. They are referred to in the Bible, in Homer's works and in Sanskrit, though with words quite unrelated to the Latin *unio,* the French *oignon,* and the Old English *unyon.* Spanish explorers and settlers introduced onions to the Western Hemisphere with phenomenal success.

Nero was reputed to crave leeks, which he believed made his voice stronger for historic orations. Leeks later became the battle symbol of Wales. Welsh regiments are even now given leeks by the Queen to wear in their hat bands as reminders of their past history.

Chives, still found wild in Italy and Greece, are an excellent species of onion to grow for both ornamental and culinary purposes. They are perfect for a graceful corner planting where they can be easily picked, even on rainy days, for snipping into attractive garnishes

CHIVES
Allium schoenoprasum
Perennial, bulbous ground cover
6 to 8 inches in height
Fast grower
Propagate from seed or division
Sun
Hardy
Leaves, flowers and bulbs eaten
Flowers in summer if not
cut back
Harvest in summer
Pink-purple flowers

Chives

and as a delicate seasoning. They are most easily raised from offsets of the larger plants by dividing them in early spring and planting 10 inches apart in sandy, weed-free, well-drained soil. Chives prefer a little shade to make them more tender and should be lifted, divided and replanted about every three years to prevent overcrowding. It pays to work over the soil well before planting and remove weeds and grass as necessary before they become integral parts of the chive clumps. Otherwise, little care besides watering is required, for chives do not easily succumb to common pests.

Enjoy chives on the table mostly in the spring and early summer, then let the more visible clumps, at least, delight you with their blossoms by allowing them to grow untouched.

The culinary uses of chives are endless. Easy to cultivate, they can be clipped back frequently during the peak growing season and added to a variety of foods for flavor and color. The young leaves of the chive plant are the only ones that should be used; the stems on which the flowers bloom are too tough. Because of this, blooming should be discouraged to insure a steady crop of young, tender shoots until the growing season begins to wane. Chives add flavor to either cooked or uncooked foods, and as a garnish add vibrant color. Use in steamed Swiss chard with chervil, in croquettes, cooked beans, cheese fondue and jellied chicken aspic. Chop up some stems and blossoms and add them to omelettes and salads, or combine the chopped stems with mint and parsley in a white bean salad. Use finely chopped chives as a garnish for cream soups and chowders; add them to hollandaise sauce for color.

Less commonly grown are garlic chives, *A. tuberosom.* Also known as Chinese chives, they impart only a faint flavor of garlic, and their stems, though tougher, can be used in many of the same ways in which the more common chives are used.

If you have a prolific crop of chive or garlic chive plants, pull some of them so the bulbs can be used as you would green onions. Chop them and fry with bacon bits to complement mashed potatoes. If your crop is too small to pull the plants, substitute green onions for the chive bulbs and green onions and garlic for the garlic chive bulbs in the recipes that follow.

POTATO GARLIC SPREAD

Cook until soft in:
water to cover
1 pound unpeeled new potatoes
4 garlic cloves
1/2 teaspoon salt
1/4 teaspoon white pepper
Drain and reserve liquid. Peel
potatoes and mash potatoes and
garlic. Combine in blender with:
4 tablespoons potato water
finely chopped raw garlic to taste
Blend until smooth, at low
speed, and gradually add:
6 to 8 tablespoons olive oil
1 tablespoon white wine vinegar
Stir in:
1 to 2 tablespoons finely chopped
    garlic chives
Adjust seasonings and transfer to
serving bowl. Cover and chill at
least 2 hours. Garnish with:
prawns
parsley sprigs
Serve with thin dark rye crisp
crackers or as sauce for fish or
vegetables.
Makes a generous 1/2 pint

PRAWNS WITH GORGONZOLA AND CHIVES

Shell and devein:
2 pounds medium-size raw prawns
Turning constantly, sauté
prawns in:
4 tablespoons butter
until they just start to turn pink.
Then add:
4 tablespoons finely chopped
    parsley
1/2 teaspoon salt
1/4 teaspoon freshly ground
    white pepper
1/4 teaspoon paprika
Cook and stir 1 or 2 minutes more.
Do not overcook. Add:
4 to 6 tablespoons dry sherry
Sprinkle with:
2 to 3 ounces Gorgonzola
    cheese, crumbled
4 tablespoons finely chopped
    chives
Toss lightly and serve immediately on:
rice or toast
Serves 4 to 6

Chives

CHIVE-CHEESE SPREAD

Combine:
8 ounces cream cheese, softened
2 ounces butter, softened
2 tablespoons finely chopped
 chives or garlic chives
1 tablespoon double cream
1/2 teaspoon Dijon-style mustard
1/4 teaspoon salt
1/8 teaspoon freshly ground
 white pepper
1 teaspoon each anchovy paste
 and paprika
Adjust seasonings to taste and
chill. Mound in center of large
round serving platter. Sprinkle
with:
paprika
finely chopped chives
Arrange around cheese:
small firm lettuce heart cups
Fill cups with choice of:
drained capers or pickled
 nasturtium seedpods
 (page 126)
finely chopped spring onions
finely chopped radishes
finely chopped green pepper
finely chopped red pepper
finely chopped black olives
Garnish with:
parsley sprigs
Serve with:
melba toast, bland crackers
Makes 30 small servings
64

OYSTER BEEF

Slice very thinly on diagonal,
against grain:
1 pound skirt steak
Coat meat with a mixture of:
1 tablespoon each cornflour and
 sake or dry sherry
1/2 teaspoon salt
2 tablespoons water
3 tablespoons finely chopped
 chive or garlic chive bulbs
In wok or iron sauté pan heat:
2 tablespoons corn oil
Add meat mixture and stir fry
2 to 3 minutes. Add:
2 tablespoons oyster sauce*
1/2 teaspoon sugar
Mix well and cook 1 minute more.
Serve over rice with garnish of:
coriander sprigs
Serves 4

*Found in some Chinese provi-
sion stores.

SPAGHETTI WITH CHIVE SAUCE

Sauté 5 minutes in:
6 tablespoons butter
6 ounces garlic chive bulbs
 and some tops
1-1/2 teaspoons chopped thyme
Add and mix well:
5 8-ounce cans mussels, finely
 chopped and drained (reserve
 liquid)
Boil until just tender in:
salted water
2 teaspoons corn oil
1-1/2 pounds spaghetti
Drain and toss in while hot,
using 2 forks:
chive bulb mixture
3/4 pint sour cream
3/4 pint reserved mussel liquid
Season to taste with:
salt
freshly ground white pepper
Cool and refrigerate to blend
flavors. Reheat slowly in heavy
non-stick pan or double boiler,
stirring with forks and adding
if too thick:
liquid mussel or chicken stock
creamy milk
Just before serving toss in:
about 3 ounces chopped chives
Transfer to heated serving
platter and sprinkle with:
6 to 8 tablespoons chopped chives
Serves 8 to 10

CHRYSANTHEMUM
Chrysanthemum
species and cultivars
Perennial suitable for bedding
1 to 5 feet in height
Fast grower
Propagate from cuttings or
division
Sun; shade in warmer areas
Needs protection from frost;
or overwinter indoors
Flowers eaten
Flowers in late summer or autumn
Various colors

Chrysanthemum

(*Chrysanthemum* species and cultivars)

While we must acknowledge the efforts of European gardeners for many of our flowers, it is the Orient that must be thanked for the tremendous developments made in the chrysanthemums grown today. So much plant breeding has been done over the years, it is almost impossible to track down the wild species to which the current garden plant owes its origin. The forms common today are the *C. morifolium* and *C. sinense.* The name chrysanthemum derives from the Greek—*chrysos* meaning gold and *anthos,* flower.

Members of the *Compositae* family along with the aster, daisy and dandelion, chrysanthemums were cultivated in China about 500 B.C. and were first taken to Japan in 800 A.D. Brought to Europe

Chrysanthemum

in 1688, they didn't survive there until a Captain Blanchard of Marseilles brought hardy plants from China to France in 1789. These plants were later introduced in England in 1808 as garden and greenhouse plants. The Royal Horticultural Society sent Robert Fortune to China in 1843 where he obtained the outdoor, autumn-flowering varieties now so famous in both Europe and America after extensive development by intrigued plant breeders.

Chrysanthemums ask only for reasonable garden soil, a share of the sun, a good meal every six weeks during the growing season and moderate watering. In colder climates they should be lifted and stored in a frost-free area for the winter and given a minimum of water. Planted out in the spring they are favorites of snails and slugs and require protection. If they are able to survive outdoors, the chrysanthemum benefits from being lifted in late summer or early autumn and divided. Remove the old woody parts and plant back the young green shoots. Cuttings can be taken in the spring and rooted in sandy soil.

Chrysanthemums have been grown for centuries in the Orient for their beauty and their use in the kitchen. The best-known recipe is the firepot or Oriental chafing dish which features the leaves. Because *C. morifolium* has a different taste than the chrysanthemum common in the Orient, many western recipes use only the more flavorful petals of the flower. The leaves of *C. morifolium* can be eaten, however, and are good cooked with other greens and soy sauce and served over rice. Japanese chrysanthemum leaves are sold in Japanese markets.

Pick the flowers before the sun is on them, wash thoroughly but gently and pull off the petals, removing the appendage attached to the flower base. Pat petals dry and refrigerate in a plastic bag until ready to use. If using in salads, blanch one second, drain and dry, and always add a tiny bit of sugar or honey. Add to fruit, green or potato salads, to chicken and orange salad or substitute for violets in violet salad adding one-half teaspoon honey to the dressing. Chrysanthemum petals give flavor and color to cream soups, fish or fowl chowders, cream or clear spinach or sorrel soup, or hard-boiled eggs, poultry or ham in cream sauce. They may also be used in almost any way in which calendulas are. Be careful not to overcook chrysanthemums as they will become bitter and lose their texture.

CHRYSANTHEMUM BALLS

Soften in lukewarm water:
1 ounce bean thread noodles*
Drain, cut into 1/2-inch lengths
and combine with:
**6 ounces finely chopped raw
  prawns**
1 egg white, slightly beaten
2 teaspoons cornflour
**1/4 teaspoon each salt and
  finely chopped garlic**
**1/8 teaspoon freshly ground
  white pepper**
**4 tablespoons finely chopped
  chrysanthemum petals**
Chill and form into 1-inch balls.
Deep fry until golden in:
salad oil
Drain on paper towels and serve
immediately with:
soy sauce
sake or dry sherry
finely chopped ginger root
Makes approximately 20 balls

*Available from some Chinese
  provision stores.

CHRYSANTHEMUM
LENTIL CAKES

Bring to gentle boil:
3/4 pint rich beef stock
6 ounces lentils
Cover and cook 45 minutes or
until lentils are soft. Remove
cover and cook over medium
high heat until almost all
moisture has evaporated. Mash
and blend in:
**5 tablespoons finely chopped
  mild onion**
**6 to 8 tablespoons finely chopped
  chrysanthemum petals**
**salt, freshly ground black pepper
  and cayenne pepper to taste**
Chill and form into 12 2-1/2-inch
flat patties. Dip in:
beaten egg
Coat with:
fine bread crumbs
Chill again. Just before serving
brown on both sides in:
corn oil
Serve as accompaniment to beef
stew or other meat and gravy
dish.
Serves 6

Cornelian Cherry

(Cornus mas)

A delightful native of Europe, this variety of dogwood has been grown for centuries for its grand yellow flowers blooming on the previous season's wood before new leaves appear. Its olive-shaped, scarlet fruit, though not too freely borne, add splashes of color in the late summer and early autumn and have a tart, delicate flavor. The leaves resemble the hazel or filbert and are an excellent foil for summer perennials. The Cornelian cherry can be either a large shrub (spreading untidily unless well pruned) or a small tree up to 25 feet high with hard, horn-like, long-lasting wood. There are several varieties, including some with variegated leaves.

Cornus mas is easily propagated by layering. Place a low-growing branch in the ground, forming a right-angle bend. Nick the stem at the bend and cover with soil mixed with a little sand. After rooting, detach and treat as a young plant. If planting a small tree, plant to the depth equal that in the nursery's container.

Any good, well-drained garden soil in a sunny location is suitable. In especially sunny climates, *Cornus mas* will thrive in semi-shade. While resistant to most pests and diseases, watch for aphid invasion.

Little known in the culinary world, Cornelian cherry fruit have a lovely tangy flavor when cooked down into a sauce, adding orange juice and lemon juice during the last few minutes of cooking time. As an accompaniment to lamb, game or poultry, the sauce adds not only flavor but a deep-red color. This fruit also makes an excellent glaze for ham, topping for ice cream, dessert omelette filling and sauce for rice pudding. In Turkey, the Cornelian cherry is used as a flavoring for sorbets; in Norway for a distilled spirit. If time is taken to pit them before cooking, they make an unusual tart or sweetmeat.

PORK FILLET WITH CORNELIAN CHERRY SAUCE

Marinate, omitting lavender cotton:

pork fillet as directed on page 118

Scrape off marinade, dry and sprinkle with salt and pepper. Brown on all sides in:

4 tablespoons butter

Transfer pork to baking dish and to frying pan add:

4 tablespoons water

2 tablespoons dry vermouth

Pour over fillet and bake, basting often, in 325° oven 20 minutes. Combine, heat and pour over baked pork:

1/2 pint Cornelian cherry sauce
4 tablespoons water

Basting often, continue baking 20 minutes or more depending upon thickness of fillet.

Transfer to heated platter and add to baking dish if desired:

additional Cornelian cherry sauce

Heat and pour over roast.

Serves 4

CORNELIAN CHERRY SAUCE

Place in heavy saucepan:
6 cups Cornelian cherry fruit
Cover, and cook over low heat
until juices start to flow. Stirring
occasionally, cook until very
soft. Remove pits and mash.
Return to heat and add:
1-1/2 cups sugar
Cook and stir 5 minutes and add:
1/4 cup orange juice
1 tablespoon lemon juice
Reheat and adjust flavors. If too
thick add a little water.
Makes approximately 2 cups

CORNELIAN CHERRY
Cornus mas
Deciduous shrub or tree
To 25 feet in height
Fast grower
Propagate from cuttings or seed
Sun
Hardy
Fruit eaten
Flowers in very early spring
Harvest in late summer
Bears when few years old
Yellow flowers, red fruit

Cornelian Cherry

RABBIT PIE

Marinate 2 hours in:
3 tablespoons lemon juice
**1 2-1/2- to 3-pound rabbit, cut
  up and skinned**
Dry rabbit and coat with:
**flour seasoned with salt, white
  pepper and paprika**
Brown on all sides in:
**4 tablespoons rendered chicken
  fat and/or butter**
Add and cook until rabbit is
almost tender:
1-1/4 pints chicken stock
4 sprigs thyme
3 bay leaves
Remove rabbit and if desired cut
meat from bones. Transfer to
deep pie dish or casserole (about
8 inches square). To stock add
and cook until almost tender
choice of:
sliced mushrooms
sliced runner beans
asparagus, cut up
**sliced unpeeled white or red
  potatoes**
small white onions

Remove vegetables to pie dish,
cool, cover and refrigerate. Discard thyme sprigs and bay, pour
stock into jar, cool, cover and
refrigerate. Next day remove fat
from stock and melt, adding
to make 4 tablespoons
rendered chicken fat or butter
Cook until bubbly and sprinkle
with:
4 tablespoons flour
Cook and stir 3 minutes and
gradually add:
3/4 pint reserved stock
scant 1/2 pint creamy milk
Cook and stir until thickened and
thin to desired consistency with:
stock
Season to taste with:
salt, white pepper and nutmeg
Heat casserole in 350° oven while
making pastry topping.

Sift:
4-1/2 ounces unbleached flour
1/2 teaspoon baking powder
**1/4 teaspoon each salt and
  baking soda**
Cut in:
1/2 ounce butter
Add:
**finely chopped herb of choice:
  thyme, parsley, rosemary, to
  taste**
With fork stir in to make
workable pastry:
5 tablespoons or more sour cream
Form into ball. Remove casserole
from oven; sprinkle liberally with:
finely chopped chives
On floured board, roll pastry to
fit casserole and place on top,
fluting edges slightly. Make 5 or
6 slits in top and bake in 375°
oven 20 minutes or until just
starting to turn golden. Fill each
slit with:
**2 teaspoons Cornelian cherry
  sauce**
Continue baking 5 minutes
longer. Cool 5 minutes before
serving.
Serves 4

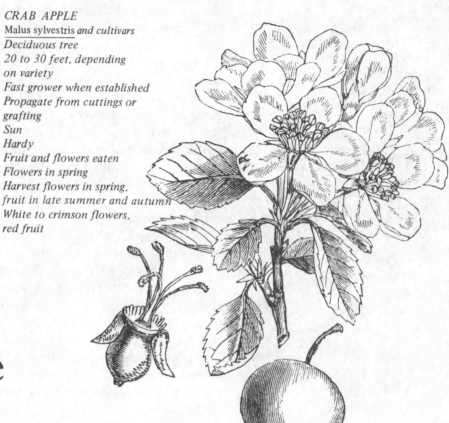

CRAB APPLE
Malus sylvestris *and cultivars*
Deciduous tree
20 to 30 feet, depending
on variety
Fast grower when established
Propagate from cuttings or
grafting
Sun
Hardy
Fruit and flowers eaten
Flowers in spring
Harvest flowers in spring,
fruit in late summer and autumn
White to crimson flowers,
red fruit

Crab Apple

(*Malus sylvestris* and cultivars)

The apple tempted Eve. Aphrodite was given a "golden" apple when she won the first beauty contest. European Stone Age dwellers ate fresh apples for dessert, and cut and sun-dried them for winter use. That the apple was long in cultivation is proven by Pliny mentioning 22 varieties, and it is thought that the Romans introduced the apple to England where it formed an important part of the wassail bowl and the tree itself was serenaded at Christmas. Farmers placed hot cakes on the branches and threw cider over them after taking a good draught and toasting: "Here's to thee old apple tree, whence thou may'st bud and whence thou may'st bloom. Hats full! and my pockets full, huzza!" Only trees that bore well were so honored to the accompani-

Crab Apple

ment of firing pistols and loud shouts. Early American settlers brought seedlings with them and established apple orchards around their villages long before John Chapman (Johnny Appleseed) roamed Ohio and Indiana in the early 1800's spreading the Gospel and giving out appleseeds.

The ancestor of all the cultivated apples in commerce today is *Malus sylvestris,* the crab apple, which still grows wild in much of Europe. It is estimated that 2000 varieties of apple are now grown, mostly in cooler climates where they reach perfection. The apple does not come true from seed, though, so that while there were many thousands of seedlings sown and grown, the modern production of apples came to the fore only when selections were made and the best varieties were propagated asexually or by vegetative means.

Crab apple trees are selected more for their shape, colorful flowers or decorative fruit, than their prodigious harvest, though it is possible to have a good crop. Your nurseryman can help you select the variety that is suited to your area as well as your preference for emphasis on flowers or fruit or a combination of both. Most varieties do not exceed a height of 30 feet.

All young apple trees need constant care and hard pruning to keep the branches well spaced and to promote outward growth (at the expense of the flowers). Later you'll be rewarded by a more beautiful tree and a proliferation of blossoms and fruit. Then only light pruning will be necessary.

Problems include fungi, insects and scale, but most can be controlled with appropriate winter spraying while still dormant. Plant in good, well-drained soil partially sheltered from the wind, preferably on a slope instead of a sinkhole where late frost may destroy early spring flowers. Plant the tree no lower than the depth it was in the container from the nursery. Suckers may get out of hand unless removed at the point they arise from the root. Don't just cut them at surface level, but rather dig if necessary and remove them roughly.

The small, attractive crab apple can be used in cooking much like other apples. When using whole, leave the stem on and cut out the blossom end. If using them sliced, chopped or grated, treat them as you would large apples.

SERVING HINTS

• For an hors d'oeuvre, core the crab apples, stuff with a mild cheese such as Cheddar and encase in pastry to make a ball. Bake in a 400° oven 15 minutes, or until the pastry is golden.

• For breakfast, brown pork link sausages, remove them from the pan and add sliced crab apples to it. Cook a few minutes, adding some brown sugar to taste. Return the sausages to the pan, heat and serve.

• Cook crab apples in an onion cream sauce flavored with calvados and serve with sweetbreads garnished with mushrooms.

• Grate the apples and combine with flaked crab meat in very thick cream for a dip. Or omit the cream for a sandwich filling on thinly sliced bread.

• Substitute for apples in chutney or in pie sliced with cinnamon, nutmeg, ginger and cloves.

CRAB APPLE FLOWERS

The flowers of the crab apple are also edible. Treat them like elderberry flowers (page 90), either dipped in batter, deep fried and served sprinkled with sugar, or added to fritter batter.

TURKEY AND CRAB APPLE CRÊPES

Prepare double recipe crêpe batter, page 150.
Cover and refrigerate at least 2 hours.
Sauté until soft in:
2 tablespoons rendered chicken fat
4 tablespoons chopped chive or garlic chive bulbs (page 62)
Add and brown slightly:
1 pound minced turkey
1/4 pound chopped mushrooms
Season with:
1/4 to 1/2 teaspoon curry powder
1/2 teaspoon salt
1/4 teaspoon freshly ground black pepper
1/2 to 1 teaspoon finely chopped sage
Cook and stir 3 minutes to blend flavors. Remove from heat and blend in:
scant 1/2 pint grated crab apples
Adjust seasonings and cool. Fill crêpes as directed and place in buttered shallow baking dish.
Tuck around crêpes:
20 whole crab apples
Top with:
2 ounces grated sharp Cheddar cheese
Bake in 400° oven until heated through and cheese is melted.
Makes 20 crêpes

Crab Apple

**LAMB KIDNEYS WITH
SPICY CRAB APPLE JELLY**

Wash:
1 pound lamb kidneys
Remove any fat and membrane, place on edge and halve lengthwise. Cut each half into thirds and place in bowl. Cover with:
ice water
2 tablespoons vinegar
Let stand 30 minutes; drain thoroughly and set aside.
Sauté until starting to turn golden in:
2 tablespoons butter
3/4 pound onions finely chopped
Sprinkle with:
2 tablespoons flour
Cook and stir 3 minutes. Add kidneys and:
2 tablespoons butter
Cook and stir over medium heat 1 minute. Then add:
1/4 pint good quality dry sherry
**1/4 teaspoon each salt and freshly
ground white pepper**

Continue cooking, turning kidneys often, 6 to 8 minutes, adding to make gravy consistency:
lamb or other meat stock
Just before serving stir in:
**3 tablespoons spicy crab apple
jelly (following)**
Sprinkle with:
finely chopped parsley
Serve with extra jelly.
Serves 6 to 8

SPICY CRAB APPLE JELLY

Combine:
**4 cups halved or quartered
crab apples**
2 cups water
2 teaspoons pickling spice
**1/4 to 1/2 teaspoon pumpkin pie
spice***
Follow directions on page 59 for making jelly, using:
2 cups sugar
*Use a mixture of 4 parts each ground cinnamon and nutmeg to 2 parts ground ginger and 1 part ground cloves.

FIDGET PIE

Combine:
**1 pound well-seasoned pork
    sausage meat**
1 tablespoon cornflour
2 tablespoons water
Place one-third of meat mixture
in bottom of shallow baking dish.
Grate separately:
1 onion
**20 to 30 crab apples (to
    make a scant 1/2 pint)**
1 large potato, peeled
Layer half the onion, apple and
potato on meat. Sprinkle with:
1 tablespoon chopped chives
Repeat layers, ending with meat.
Cover and bake in 350° oven
20 minutes; uncover and continue baking until potatoes
are done and top is crispy.
Sprinkle with:
finely chopped parsley
Serves 4

SPICED CRAB APPLES

In heavy saucepan combine:
1 pound sugar
**1/2 pint white vinegar or
    white wine vinegar**
4 tablespoons water
2 lemon slices
1 tablespoon whole cloves
1 4-inch stick cinnamon, broken
3 slices ginger root, or
1/2 teaspoon whole allspice
Stir to dissolve sugar, bring to
boil and cook over medium heat
10 minutes. Cool slightly.
With tines of small fork prick
in several places:
6 cups crab apples
Add to syrup and over medium
heat bring temperature of syrup
to 180°. Turning apples often and
maintaining 180° temperature,
cook 10 minutes. Pour into hot
sterilized jars and seal. Cool and
store in dark area at least 2 weeks
before using. Serve as garnish for
meat or poultry dishes. Strained
leftover syrup is excellent on
vanilla ice cream.
Fills approximately 3 half-
pint jars

CRAB APPLE GLACÉ

Dip in:
glacé syrup (page 30)
crab apples
Place 1 inch apart on baking
sheets and bake in 325° oven 8
minutes or until slightly softened. Cool on rack and serve
as garnish for meat, poultry
or game dishes.

Cranberry

(Vaccinium macrocarpum and

CRANBERRY
Vaccinium macrocarpum
and cultivars
Sometimes deciduous, perennial
creeping shrub
Fast grower
Propagate from cuttings or layers
Sun, if moisture available
Hardy
Berries eaten
Flowers in summer
Harvest in autumn
White flowers, red berries

The genus *Vaccinium,* which includes both the cranberry and blueberry, may have been named after the cow *(L. vacca),* an animal that once foraged far and wide among herbs and berries. More definitely known is that long-legged cranes dining on large, red, somewhat bitter, wild berries in swampy areas gave their name to cranberries (crane berries) and that they grow in both America *(V. macrocarpum)* and in Europe *(V. oxycoccus).*

Growing wild from Nova Scotia to North Carolina and west to Wisconsin, the *V. macrocarpum* berries were long known to the Indians. They were later adopted by the Pilgrims for jellies and sauces and as an accompaniment to the wild turkey that became traditional at once-a-year Thanksgiving feasts. History also records that cranberries were a form of preventive medicine on long whaling voyages. Successfully stored in wooden barrels filled with cold water, the cranberries were served to the crew members to ward off scurvy. The wild blueberry, *V. angustifolium,* was also harvested by the Indians and combined with venison for the making of pemmican.

Captain Henry Hall, a Revolutionary War veteran, began domestic cultivation of the cranberry in the early 1800's in the town of Dennis on Cape Cod. More recently, commercial cultivation has broadened, for cranberry juice, with its distinctive flavor and high vitamin C content, has become a year-round beverage. The chief commercial growing areas in North America are in New Jersey, Wisconsin, Washington, Oregon, Massachusetts, near Vancouver in British Columbia and near Drummondville in Quebec.

Wet ground is essential for growing cranberries, but their cousins the blueberries are equally attractive and thrive under drier conditions in good soil, but it must be peaty and acid. Both are easily propagated from dormant cuttings taken in the winter for spring rooting in

& Blueberry

Vaccinium corymbosum and cultivars)

peat and sand. Severe winter pruning of most but not all the older canes is desirable. Flowers and fruit are produced on young growth from the previous year's wood, so a balance must be struck between bushiness and fruit production. Vacciniums are hardy and generally free from pests and diseases. Watch for rust and use a winter fungicide spray, if necessary.

Cranberries are ready to pick in autumn when they separate easily from the bush. Their natural waxy coating protects the berry from spoilage, so they store well to be enjoyed for some time. When the berry does become overripe, its brilliant color will turn dull and its juices will begin to seep through the protective skin.

Wash cranberries thoroughly and remove stems before serving. They combine well with celery, apples, raisins and oranges, and with seasonings such as cinnamon, cloves and nutmeg. They can be made into a dressing for salads, a sauce, marmalade, relish, conserve or sorbet. Add them to stuffing for pork or fowl, or to pork sausage meat for grilled patties. Prepare a glaze for ham or fowl, or a cranberry topping for cheesecake or ice cream. Make a mould with sweetened cranberry juice, gelatinous chicken broth and bits of leftover chicken of turkey. And, for an interesting and unusual combination, add cranberries to cold borshch.

Blueberries are high in vitamin A and low in calories. They are best eaten fresh, plain with cream and a little sugar. But they can be added to or made into what seems like an endless number of dishes: fritters, pancakes, pudding, trifle, sorbet, custard, shortcake, pies, American "grunts", sauces, stuffing, jam, jelly and conserve. For a refreshing salad, combine cottage cheese and blueberries and serve with a honey, lemon and oil dressing. Blueberries freeze well. Wash and dry them thoroughly, freeze on baking sheets, bag and seal.

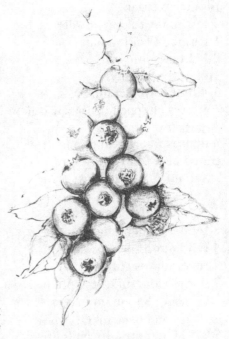

BLUEBERRY
Vaccinium corymbosum
and cultivars
Branching, deciduous shrub
4 to 12 feet in height
Fast grower
Propagate from cuttings
Sun; shade in warmer areas
Hardy
Berries eaten
Flowers in spring
Harvest in late summer and autumn
White-tinted pink flowers,
blue berries

77

Cranberry & Blueberry

CRANBERRY BREAD

Sift together:
1 pound unbleached flour
14 ounces sugar
4 teaspoons baking powder
1 teaspoon baking soda
2-1/2 teaspoons salt
Mix in thoroughly:
3/4 pint halved cranberries
**4 ounces chopped pecans or wal-
nuts (optional)**
4 ounces fine wheat germ
**grated peel from 4 large oranges
(about 6 tablespoons)**
Combine:
2 eggs, slightly beaten
8 fluid ounces orange juice
4 fluid ounces warm water
2 fluid ounces corn oil
Stir into flour mixture until just
moistened. Spoon into 2 greased
loaf tins and bake in 350° oven
50 to 60 minutes. Bread is done
when loaf pulls away from sides of
pan. Cool on rack 5 minutes and
turn out on to rack.
Makes 2 loaves

POT ROAST
WITH CRANBERRIES

Sprinkle with:
flour and salt
**1 4-pound joint rolled topside
or silverside**
In a heavy ovenproof casserole or
Dutch oven brown the meat on
all sides in:
**1 tablespoon rendered beef fat or
corn oil**
Remove joint and in the same pan
brown:
**4 tablespoons each diced onion,
carrot and celery with leaves**
1/2 teaspoon sugar
Add:
**5 tablespoons each dry red wine
and beef stock**
1/2 teaspoon salt
**1/4 teaspoon freshly ground
black pepper**

Return meat to casserole. Cover,
lower heat and cook slowly 1-1/2
hours or until meat is almost
tender, adding more stock if
needed. Then add:
**2 tablespoons frozen concen-
trated orange juice**
1 teaspoon sugar
**1/2 teaspoon Worcestershire
sauce**
6 to 8 ounces cranberries
Cover and cook 7 minutes until
cranberries are soft. Remove meat
and force juices and vegetables
through sieve or food mill back
into the casserole. Slice meat,
return to sauce and cook, covered,
5 to 10 minutes. Adjust seasonings and transfer to heated serving platter. Sprinkle with:
**4 tablespoons finely chopped
parsley**
Serve with rice, barley or
mashed or baked potatoes.
Serves 4 to 6

Cranberry & Blueberry

BLUEBERRY STUFFING FOR POULTRY

Cook, covered, until soft in:
4 tablespoons butter
5 tablespoons each finely chopped onion and celery with leaves
1/2 teaspoon each finely chopped thyme and marjoram
1/4 teaspoon finely chopped sage
Toss in:
2-1/2 to 3 ounces unseasoned croûtons
4 tablespoons milk
Season to taste with:
poultry seasoning
salt and pepper
Toss in:
2 ounces blueberries (more if desired)
Makes enough for a 3-pound chicken

BLUEBERRY SOUP

In heavy saucepan combine:
2 cups blueberries
1 cup water
1/4 cup sugar
1 2-inch stick cinnamon
6 slices lemon or lime
1/2 teaspoon allspice
Cook over medium heat and stir to dissolve sugar. Bring to gentle boil and, stirring occasionally, cook 15 minutes until berries are soft. Force through sieve, pressing as much pulp through as possible. Add to sieved blueberries:
1/4 cup red wine, mixed with
1 teaspoon arrowroot
Cook and stir until thickened. Cool and refrigerate at least 4 hours until very cold. Beat in:
1/4 pint sour cream
Adjust with more wine or sour cream and serve in chilled bowls with garnish of:
tiny white violets
Serves 4 to 6

BLUEBERRY TORTONI

Beat until stiff:
1 egg white
Gradually beat in until satiny:
2 tablespoons castor sugar
Wash beaters and whip:
8 fluid ounces double cream
Gradually beat in:
2 tablespoons castor sugar
1 teaspoon rose water, violet water or vanilla essence
Fold into egg white and freeze until edges are solid. Stir with fork and fold in:
3 cups (about 1-1/4 pints) blueberries
Return to freezer until mixture begins to set.
Spoon into 8 chilled glass bowls or stem glasses. Decorate if desired with:
violet flowers
Serves 8

Currant

(*Ribes* species and cultivars)

Currants were named for their resemblance to the small seedless grapes that grow around Corinth (Middle English—*raysons of Courante,* raisins of ancient Corinthia). However, this fruit has a unique acidy tang quite unlike the taste of raisins. Unfortunately, currant bushes are hosts for a life stage of the blister fungus which plays havoc with white pines. Because of this, the United States government has tried to eradicate the bush in areas where the pines grow, thus jeopardizing their popularity. The black currant, *R. nigrum,* the red currant and white currant, *R. sativum,* are all important commercial crops in Europe. In the United States, the native currant, *R. sanguineum,* has been in cultivation only about 100 years. It also grows wild in many areas on the West Coast, and its loose red flower clusters, or panicles, are a sight to behold in the spring.

The Rocky Mountain Indians of North America used all varieties of currants, but preferred the black currant dried for making pemmican. They also ate them raw, cooked into a soup or dried as a seasoning for stews. Currant leaves were steeped in boiling water, strained, honey was added and the mixture was boiled into a syrup.

Currant bushes prefer moist conditions and can stand heavy, rather wet soil. They will tolerate sun, but prefer the high shade of their native woods. Cuttings in the winter root easily in sandy soil and should be taken from a bush that bears well. Otherwise buy a good

Currant

CURRANT
Ribes *species and cultivars*
Sometimes evergreen bush or shrub
8 to 12 feet in height
Fast grower
Propagate from cuttings
Shade
Hardy
Berries eaten
Flowers in spring
Harvest in summer
Red or white flowers

plant from your nurseryman, who can recommend one or more of the many different crosses.

Prune in autumn to remove shoots that have already produced fruit and to encourage growth of new canes. Feed with heavy dressings of well-rotted compost. Currants are attacked by rusts and should be protected while dormant with a fungicide. If after a good number of years plants appear leggy and do not produce young shoots, replace them. Harvest in summer for a delightful treat, a good contrast to the heavier texture of most summer fruits.

High in vitamin C with a sweet tart flavor, the currant is a member of the gooseberry family and somewhat resembles it in taste. Even when dried to be used as a flavoring, this currant is not to be confused with the dried raisin currant. Like the blueberry and raspberry, currants are best eaten raw just upon fully ripening, and are good served simply with cream and sugar. Currants freeze well. Wash, pat dry thoroughly, freeze on baking sheets, bag and seal.

As they are rich in natural pectin, ripe berries may be selected when making pure currant jelly (it is not necessary to remove all the small stems before cooking). Currants also combine well with raspberries in jelly; select slightly underripe currants for the higher concentration of pectin needed.

Currant

COOKING HINTS

• For a meat sauce, combine currant jam or jelly with brown sauce or lamb gravy seasoned with sherry or lemon juice or prepared mustard. Or combine with chutney, lemon juice, brandy and salt to taste; or with horseradish and dry mustard to taste.

• Sprinkle a currant jelly garnish with chopped mint or grated orange rind.

• Add a slice of sour apple and currant juice (page 29) to taste to red cabbage as an accompaniment to pork.

• Make a jelly from currant juice (page 29) and serve as a dessert with grape pudding (page 108) and a garnish of rose geranium leaves, candied violets or flower petals.

• Cook 1 cup currants with 1/4 cup water, 1/2 cup sugar and 1 teaspoon lemon juice; thicken with 1 to 2 teaspoons cornflour, cool and place in baked tart shells lined with softened cream cheese.

• Fold fresh currants into sweetened whipped cream until it will hold no more; freeze briefly for a light, rich dessert.

CURRANT STUFFING FOR GOOSE

Sauté until soft in:
4 tablespoons rendered goose fat
2 large onions, finely chopped
2 large stalks celery and leaves, finely chopped
Add and cook, stirring constantly, 5 minutes:
3/4 pint currants, stemmed
4 tablespoons sweet vermouth
1 teaspoon sugar
8 ounces (raw) wild rice, cooked in stock (substitute half long-grain white rice and half brown rice)
1 teaspoon salt
Cool and stuff 8-pound goose.

BAR-LE-DUC
(French Currant Jelly)

In a copper, enamel or non-stick pan, combine:
1 pound currants, stemmed and mashed
11 ounces sugar
Let stand overnight; then bring slowly to the boil and boil 3 minutes. Remove from heat and let stand (in the same pan) for 24 hours. Pour into sterilized jars, cover as usual, and store in a cool dry place. Bar-le-duc is the classic French currant jelly.

RODGROD MED FLODE

In heavy saucepan combine:
2 cups each red currants, red raspberries and pitted and halved cherries
1 2-inch stick cinnamon
2 rose geranium leaves
Bring to slow boil, cover and cook, stirring occasionally, until fruit is soft. Discard cinnamon and geranium leaves and force fruit through sieve. Add:
1 cup (about 7 ounces) sugar
2-1/2 tablespoons cornflour dissolved in
4 tablespoons cold water
Cook and stir until thickened. Adjust with:
sugar to taste
While hot pour into crystal serving bowl and to prevent skin from forming sprinkle lightly with:
sugar
Cool, cover and refrigerate until very cold.
Serve with:
plain or whipped double cream
Serves 8

Douglas Fir

(Pseudotsuga menziesii)

Reaching heights of over 200 feet in the forests of Oregon and Washington, the stately Douglas fir is one of North America's most impressive trees, well known for the volume of strong timber it provides. Its beauty in gardens has made it popular wherever climate and space are favorable, and its variations are numerous: blue foliage, weeping shapes and fastigiate forms with erect and parallel branches. These are all grafted plants and are available from nurseries. Seed plantings usually produce only the typical tree. After many years of growth, the Douglas fir rarely grows taller than 75 feet outside its native habitat.

The tree was named after David Douglas, a Scottish botanist and traveller, who first sent seed back to England in 1827 from the dense forests of North America. Douglas experienced great difficulty in obtaining the seeds. The trunks were too huge for his puny hatchet, the cones so high even buckshot would not dislodge them. But finally he succeeded, returning to England with cones containing the precious seeds from which the tree could be propagated.

DOUGLAS FIR
Pseudotsuga menziesii
Evergreen tree
To 100 feet in height
Fast grower
Propagate from seed
Sun
Hardy
Young tips of shoots eaten
Harvest in spring

Douglas Fir

Recently botanists, sometimes capricious, have decided to change the name to *Pseudotsuga menziesii* after another Scotsman, Archibald Menzies. He had sent back dried specimens of this fir some years before Douglas had sent the cones. Menzies, a famous botanist and skilled surgeon, had been instructed by the Royal Society to obtain for study dried specimens of all plants encountered while on a round-the-world voyage of the "Discovery," captained by George Vancouver. Though a plant can be named after the person who first sends back specimens, Menzies was probably originally slighted because propagation was not possible with his dried specimens and the honor went to Douglas. Botanists are fascinated with Menzies, his family's botanical fame, his studies at Edinburgh's Royal Botanic Garden and his fabulous reputation as a surgeon in the Royal Navy.

Propagation of the Douglas fir is difficult from cuttings, but seeds taken in autumn germinate easily when placed in a pot or pan of well-rotted leaf mould and sand. Firm the soil, sow seeds thinly and well spaced, and cover to a depth of half an inch. In a cool, wet garden area sink the pots in the ground to help keep them moist. When stems reach the size of matchsticks in the spring, transplant each one to a three-inch pot in a mixture of one-third each leaf mould, sand and soil. At nine- to 10-inches height, seedlings are ready for transfer to gallon cans or eight-inch pots. After rooting well they can be planted in permanent roomy locations in the garden where plenty of moisture can be provided until established.

During first years of growth prune away any surplus leaders that develop. Allow only one central shoot so that a straight trunk will form. Lower branches can be gradually removed as the tree matures, but always leave at least one-third of the branches.

Cut when young and tender, Douglas fir tips impart a subtle woodsy flavor to foods in which they are cooked. High in vitamin C, young fir tips, either fresh or dried, make a fine, unusual tea when boiled, or if soaked in cold water, a natural mouthwash. Use fir tips for dipping into marinades and basting barbecued meats or fowl, or fresh or dried for infusing stocks to be used in cooking complementary dishes.

LAMB ROAST WITH DOUGLAS FIR TIPS

Make slits in:
1 5- to 6-pound leg of lamb
Insert in each slit:
sliver of garlic clove
Sprinkle liberally with:
salt
freshly ground black pepper
Place on rack in roasting tin and surround with:
1 large carrot, sliced
1 celery stalk and leaves, chopped
Place on top of roast:
6 to 8 Douglas fir tips
Roast in 300° oven 2 hours or until lamb is cooked to taste. Remove lamb to heated platter and discard tips. Raise oven temperature to brown vegetables; then remove them with slotted spoon and save for making soup stock. Pour off almost all fat in tin and place over medium heat. Sprinkle with:
flour to absorb remaining fat
Scrape up any bits on bottom of tin, cook and stir 3 minutes. Gradually add to make thin gravy
lamb stock or water
Adjust seasonings and serve gravy in heated bowl. Sprinkle roast with:
chopped parsley and chives
Serves 8

TORTILLA* SOUP

Sauté, covered, until just starting to soften in:

3 tablespoons rendered chicken fat

1 medium onion, cut in chunks and separated

1 small green pepper, cut in chunks

1/2 teaspoon each salt and freshly ground black pepper

1/4 teaspoon or more cumin powder

Add and bring to boil:

1-1/4 pints rich Douglas fir beef or chicken stock (page 28)

Add:

3 to 4 ripe tomatoes, peeled and quartered

5 tablespoons coarsely grated Mozzarella or mild Cheddar cheese

Cook until cheese is just melted and adjust seasonings.

Just before serving add:

crisped tortillas*, broken into pieces

Serves 2 as luncheon dish

*Tortillas are thin Mexican pancakes made with pounded maize and baked on a griddle. They can sometimes be bought canned. However, if they are not available use ordinary, thin crêpes, or pappadoms, for an interesting variation.

VENISON STEW

Combine and simmer 10 minutes:

1/2 pint red wine

2 tablespoons olive oil

2 onion slices

1 celery stalk and leaves, cut up

1 carrot, sliced

2 large bay leaves, broken

4 parsley sprigs

3 or 4 thyme sprigs, or

1 or 2 rosemary sprigs

1/2 teaspoon salt

6 peppercorns, lightly crushed

Cool and add:

1-1/2 pounds venison stew meat, cut into 1-1/2-inch cubes

Stirring often, marinate 3 or more hours depending on quality and age of venison. Drain and dry meat; coat with:

flour seasoned with salt, pepper and paprika

Brown a few pieces of meat at a time on all sides in:

2 tablespoons or more rendered beef fat

Raise heat and deglaze frying pan with:

6 to 8 tablespoons red wine

Add:

scant 3/4 pint rich Douglas fir beef stock (page 28)

1/2 pound mushrooms, sliced

6 to 10 juniper berries, lightly crushed

Cover and simmer until meat is tender, adding more stock if needed. Last 10 minutes add if desired:

12 small white onions

1 green pepper, cut in chunks

Check sauce for seasonings and add:

1/4 pint sour cream (optional)

Transfer to heated platter and sprinkle with:

finely chopped parsley

Serve with wild rice or brown rice.

Serves 4

Elaeagnus

(Elaeagnus multiflora)

ELAEAGNUS
Elaeagnus multiflora
Deciduous, occasionally
evergreen shrub
6 to 10 feet in height and width
Fast grower
Propagate from cuttings
Sun or light shade
Hardy
Fruit eaten
Flowers in spring
Harvest in summer
Yellow flowers, red fruit

Handsome for its foliage alone, either as a specimen plant in a lawn or as a hedge, *Elaeagnus multiflora* flowers fragrantly in April and early May, later producing its showy fruit. Trees and shrubs of the genus *Elaeagnus* are found in many parts of the world from North America to Europe, West Asia and the Far East. While the fruit of some of these is edible, that of *E. multiflora* is the best.

Elais was the goddess who could change anything she touched into oil, and in ancient Greece oil meant olive oil. That elaeagnus is sometimes called "wild olive" and that both "olive" and "oil" derive from *elaia*, the Greek word for olive, are understandable. *Agnus* derives from *hagnos* meaning pure, and also names the "chaste tree,"

Vitex agnus-castus, a shrub of the verbena family and not related to the elaeagnus. Actually few would ever relate the elaeagnus fruit's sweet and pleasant taste to olives no matter what common parentage botanists have found in the varieties of both hemispheres.

Though seed propagation is possible, cuttings taken in mid-summer, when new growth has begun to harden, are more satisfactory and assure reproduction of desired characteristics. Exact timing is determined when a young side shoot pulled off takes with it a piece of bark. Four- to five-inch cuttings can be taken by severing with a razor blade or very sharp knife some of the shoot tip. Remove lower leaves, dip ends in a root-promoting hormone, then place in a flat of moist, sharp sand or mixture of equal parts coarse sand and moss peat. Keep until rooted in a closed greenhouse-type atmosphere so leaves stay moist (six to eight weeks); then put in small pots and place in a well-protected area until established. Plant out in a sheltered location (in the small pots or transplant to a larger container) for two seasons before replanting in a final location, not too deeply and watered well.

Plants in open, sunny spots produce fruit after three years, but the elaeagnus isn't otherwise fussy as to light or soil. As trees they can reach 20 feet, though eight to 10 feet is more common. As specimen plants or border shrubs they can be shaped, restricted and kept open by pruning in early summer and autumn. Their fragrant flowers are small and white; their berries bright red. Leaves, two-inch long, green ovals, have tufts of brown hair on their silver undersides. Young shoots are covered with attractive red-brown scales. Pests and diseases are rare for all varieties of this pretty shrub-tree.

The taste of *E. multiflora* is well suited to western palates and undoubtedly will find favor with adventuresome cooks. The fruit is ready for picking in late summer and early autumn. Clear red when ripe, the berries should readily separate from the bush; wash well, removing all the stems. Combine fresh elaeagnus berries with other fruit in an open fruit tart or serve berry-filled omelettes for dessert. Elaeagnus sauce adds flavor and color to poultry and game dishes, and makes an excellent topping for ice cream. Though the lovely red color is lost when made into jelly, the flavor is enhanced. Serve jelly in grilled cheese sandwiches or on toast.

Elaeagnus

ELAEAGNUS JELLY

In large deep saucepan combine:
4 pints elaeagnus berries
1/4 pint water
Cover and cook over medium
heat until berries are very soft.
Place in jelly bag as directed on
page 59 and continue to follow
directions, adding:
5 ounces sugar
1 teaspoon red food coloring

ELAEAGNUS SAUCE

In deep heavy saucepan combine:
1-1/2 pints elaeagnus berries
4 tablespoons water
Cover and cook over medium
heat until soft. Mash and force
through sieve, pushing through
as much pulp as possible. Add
and stir to dissolve:
5 tablespoons sugar
Bring to gentle boil, cover and
cook over medium heat, stirring
often, 10 minutes or until
thickened. Adjust with more sugar
if needed and cool.
Makes approximately 1 pint

GLAZED CORNISH HENS*

In blender purée:
5 tablespoons dry vermouth
3 tablespoons lemon or
lime juice
6 ounces chopped spring onions
and some tops
1 clove garlic, chopped
4 tablespoons chopped parsley
2 teaspoons chopped thyme
Place in shallow glass dish:
4 Cornish hens*
Pour blender contents over hens,
cover and marinate, turning
several times, 4 to 6 hours. Rub
all sides of hens with:
softened butter
Sprinkle with:
salt
freshly ground white pepper
paprika
Place hens in shallow baking tin
back side up, pour marinade over
them and bake in 325° oven 15
minutes. Turn breast side up,
baste with marinade and bake
10 minutes longer. Raise heat
slightly if hens are not browned.
Combine:
1/4 pint elaeagnus sauce
2 tablespoons each dry vermouth
and lemon or lime juice
Brush bits of marinade off hens

and coat with sauce. Return to
oven and cook, basting often, for
15 minutes. Halve and serve with
juices. Or cool, cover and refrigerate. Serve cold with garnish of:
spearmint sprigs
Serves 8

*British cooks should substitute 4
two-pound chickens or 8 poussins.
For the latter, cut the roasting
time by 5 minutes at each stage
(about 25 minutes in all).

HAM STEAK

Score edges of fat on:
1 1-1/2-pound ham steak
Marinate, turning often, for
2 hours in:
4 tablespoons dry vermouth
6 lightly crushed juniper berries
4 tablespoons chopped parsley
Remove ham, drain marinade and
combine with:
4 tablespoons melted butter
Grill ham under medium heat,
basting often, and turning once,
20 to 30 minutes depending
upon thickness of ham. Transfer
to heated platter and surround
with:
grilled pineapple rings filled
with elaeagnus sauce
Serves 4

ELDERBERRY
Sambucus nigra *and*
Sambucus caerulea
Deciduous shrub or small tree
25 to 30 feet in height
Propagate from cuttings
Sun or light shade
Hardy
Berries and flowers eaten
Flowers in spring
Harvest flowers in spring,
berries in autumn
White flowers, black or blue berries

Elderberry

(*Sambucus nigra* — European)
(*Sambucus caerulea* — American)

The ancients related the elderberry to death and sorrow. Those who slept beneath its boughs could be expected to fall into a narcotic stupor or die. Some said Judas hanged himself on an elderberry tree.

In the more recent past the elderberry was noted for its beneficial medicinal and chemical properties—berry wine for sore throats, boiled leaf broth as an insect spray, flower water to cool the skin, inner bark for burn ointments, dye from its lovely blue fruit for hair coloring and from its bark for Scottish tartans.

Early edible uses included boiled leaves, dried flower tea and a sweetened drink from boiled berries. North American Indians used the elderberry's flowers and leaves in salads. Elderberry wood was sought

Elderberry

after for "mathematical instruments." Shoots made into pipes or flutes were "more shrill," according to Pliny. And in France, elderberry shoots were used to support vines. Long considered weed trees because they seed easily and grow quickly, elderberries are especially useful and ornamental when trained as standard trees. The fruit of the American species, *S. caerulea,* is larger and juicier than that of the European, *S. nigra.*

Made in the autumn, eight- to 10-inch hard-wood cuttings root readily if taken when firm and placed in sandy loam. After one season they can be planted out almost anywhere if kept moist every spring. In windy areas they offer protection to more delicate plantings. Elderberry is almost pest and disease free.

To grow as a tree, remove all but the strongest shoot and pinch out the tip when grown to the desired height. When well established, prune to encourage bushiness and prevent overcrowding. If older trees become unruly, they can be cut back hard and vigorous stump sprouts will grow tremendously in a year.

The pea-sized, tart elderberry is high in vitamins A, B, C and in calcium, potassium and iron. Picked just as they turn a lovely bluish black, elderberries complement apples or grapes, and add color and piquancy to fruit salads and compotes. With a little lemon juice, they enhance the flavor and appearance of a peach or gooseberry pie flavored with cinnamon, cloves and nutmeg. Combined with fruit juice or with brandy, the berries, cooked with sugar, spices and a touch of lemon juice, make a flavorful, nutritional beverage. They can also be made into an unusual chutney or ketchup, and, of course, the well-known elderberry wine and jelly.

The delicately scented blossoms of *S. caerulea* are also edible and more flavorful than most flowers. Good for making wine, vinegar or syrup, they can also be dipped in batter, deep fried and served sprinkled with sugar and grated orange peel, or added to fritter, pancake and muffin batter. Green blossoms, not fully opened, can be pickled and used as a substitute for capers. Flower clusters should be picked in the early morning before the sun is on them, washed, dried and placed in a plastic bag. Allow them to "steam" in the sun and the flowers will separate from the clusters easily.

Elderberry

ELDERFLOWER SORBET

Pour over:
**1 pint firmly packed elder-
    flowers**
3/4 pint boiling water
Let stand 1 hour.
Soften in:
2 tablespoons cold water
1 envelope unflavored gelatine
Strain and discard flowers; reheat
liquid. Dissolve softened gelatine
in liquid; then stir in:
**6 tablespoons each castor sugar
    and lime juice**
Pour into 2 ice trays and freeze,
stirring occasionally with fork,
until partially frozen. Spoon into
bowl set over ice and beat with
egg beater. Gradually fold in:
2 egg whites, beaten stiff
Return to trays and freeze.
Spoon into serving dishes and
garnish with:
mint sprigs
Serve as accompaniment to pork
or other roast.
Makes 8 small servings

ELDERBERRY SOUP

Combine and cook until berries
are soft (about 40 minutes):
1-1/2 pints elderberries
 2-1/2 pints water
1 1-inch cinnamon stick
4 cloves
1 large lemon, sliced
Force through sieve, pressing as
much pulp through as possible.
Add, to make 3-1/4 pints liquid:
**unsweetened crab apple or
    grape juice (page 29)
    (if using commercial juice,
    dilute to half-strength with
    water and use less sugar)**
5 ounces sugar
Heat and stir to dissolve sugar
and cook 10 minutes. Dissolve in:
2 tablespoons cold water
1 teaspoon arrowroot
Cook and stir until thickened.
Adjust to taste with:
sugar
lemon juice
Chill at least 4 hours and serve in
chilled bowls with:
dollops of sour cream
Sprinkle lightly with:
nutmeg
Serves 6 to 8

PICKLED ELDERFLOWERS

Place in stone or glass jar:
2 cups elderflowers
Bring to boil:
1 cup cider vinegar
Pour over flowers and let stand
1 hour. Drain and reserve vinegar
for future use. Use the pickled
flowers in tossed salad.

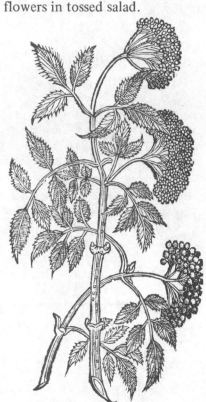

Fig

(Ficus carica and cultivars)*

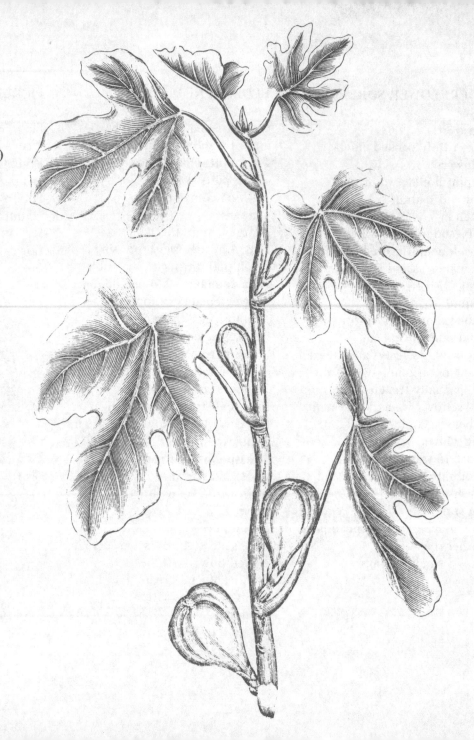

Native to the Middle East, the fig tree (*carica* from Caria, an ancient district of Asia Minor) has spread to temperate climates everywhere, not only because of its fruit, but also its fine foliage and ornamental qualities. Early introduction in Britain apparently failed because the strains weren't hardy, but Cardinal Pole's reintroduction during the 1500's in Lambeth, a borough of London, fared better.

Greatly admired for their food value, figs were a staple to the Spartans. Dried figs were discovered in the ruins of Pompeii and Pliny listed 29 varieties. The fig was dedicated to Bacchus and was used in pagan religious ceremonies. Jesus desired to eat figs on the road to Bethany, thereby making it a sacred tree to the early Christians.

The majority of fig trees grown today are female plants, and cross pollination is not needed for production of fruit. In the Middle East three crops of fruit can be expected each year; in other areas, however, only one or possibly two is the norm. Fig trees are rarely large or tall trees, though they do tend to spread.

Since the fig prefers warmth, pick your sunniest spot near a wall for shelter, if possible. Though sandy soil is preferred, stony soil or old building debris is no deterrent. It is best to have a restricted root run for prolific fruiting. Fruit are produced in pairs in the axils between the upper side of the leaf stems and the branches. Continually formed on new growth as shoots develop, fruit will ripen as branches mature. Pruning is minimal except for cutting out old branches in the winter to encourage young growth close to the main trunk. Cultivation should not be deep, and avoid adding too much nitrogen to the soil. It will promote the foliage at the expense of the fruit. To encourage more vigorous branches, pinch back a number of young shoots. The fig will also make an excellent espalier. Select the variety suited to your area. Where hard frost is a problem, trees may not develop, but shrubs will.

Most commonly eaten dried in this country, fresh figs are served as a sweet dessert and with melon as an hors d'oeuvre in parts of France and Italy. The flavor of fresh and dried figs varies according to the variety. The black fig is apt to be small, but full of rich flavor and is delicious eaten immediately upon picking. Peel ripe but firm figs carefully. Figs may be dried in the sun and stored refrigerated.

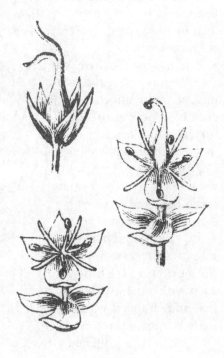

FIG
Ficus carica *and cultivars*
Deciduous tree or large shrub
15 to 30 feet in height, depending on variety
Slow grower
Propagate from cuttings or grafted plants
Sun
Not fully hardy, depending on variety
Fruit eaten
Harvest in summer and autumn

Fig

SERVING HINTS FOR FRESH FIGS

- Serve for breakfast with crisp bacon and pass the peppermill; or heat in a chafing dish with cooked pork sausages.
- For an hors d'oeuvre, cut figs into lengths and spread with a mixture of cream cheese and crumbled Gorgonzola cheese softened to a spreading consistency with double cream and Cognac to taste. Or leave whole, wrap in prosciutto or thinly sliced ham and serve with a garnish of parsley.
- Figs can be prepared in innumerable ways for dessert. Slit pockets in fresh figs, stuff each with a maraschino cherry half and chopped walnuts, marinate in rum and roll in sugar. Or soak in rum, chill and serve over vanilla ice cream with a grating of chocolate.
- For a tart, soak figs in apricot or orange liqueur, roll in sugar and place in a baked tart shell; cover with lightly whipped double cream.
- Cover chilled figs with raspberry purée mixed with sweetened whipped cream and kirsch and top with fresh whole raspberries.

94

FIG CHUTNEY

In heavy saucepan cook to dissolve sugar:

2 cups coarsely chopped black figs
5 to 6 tablespoons sugar

Add:

5 to 6 tablespoons vinegar
3 small dried red peppers, crushed
2 garlic cloves, finely chopped
1 to 2 slices ginger root, finely chopped
2 teaspoons mustard seed
1 cup raisins
1/8 teaspoon salt

Bring to gentle boil and cook, stirring often, 5 to 8 minutes to blend flavors. Figs should remain firm. Serve immediately with rice and venison or other game.

Makes approximately 1-3/4 cups

ROAST CHICKEN WITH FIGS

Combine:

4 tablespoons honey infused with rose petals or rose geraniums (page 27)
4 tablespoons softened butter
1 teaspoon salt
1/2 teaspoon freshly ground white pepper

Rub this mixture both inside and out on:

1 4-pound roasting chicken or 2 frying chickens

Roast in 425° oven until golden on all sides. Lower heat and add:

6 to 8 small white onions
2 green peppers, cut into chunks

Continue roasting, basting often, 10 to 20 minutes, depending upon size of chicken.

To pan juices add:

16 to 20 fresh figs, halved

Sprinkle all with:

3 tablespoons honey infused with rose petals or rose geraniums

Roast 15 minutes or until chicken is tender, basting often. Remove chicken, figs and vegetables to heated platter and pour juices over them. Sprinkle with:

6 to 8 tablespoons toasted slivered almonds

Serve with runner beans and brown rice.

Serves 6 to 8

Fuchsia

(*Fuchsia* species and cultivars)

Unique in that it is not a member of a larger, well-known family, the fuchsia has intrigued botanists ever since its over 100 species were discovered growing wild in Latin America and New Zealand in the 16th century. Leonard Fuchs, a German botanist, included the fuchsia in a grand book of woodcuts of plants at the time. He was later honored, in 1703, by Père Plumier, who published a description of this plant, naming it *Fuchsia triphylla flore coccineo*. Seed of this species was sent to England from Santo Domingo, becoming the first cultivated fuchsia.

Fuchs suggested the plant might be efficacious in treating the plague, though its medicinal value seems not to have been pursued since. He wrote, "It increases the pleasure and delight not a little if there is added an acquaintance with the virtues and powers of these same plants," apparently referring to something beyond its unusual beauty—perhaps its culinary as well as medicinal virtues.

Continuing introductions of different wild species in England date from 1786 when a London nurseryman, Henderson, of St. Johns Wood decided to cultivate them seriously. Soon many hybrids, fore-runners of today's varieties, were developed.

The fuchsia's colorful, bicolored, pendulous blossoms are now a familiar delight. In the United States they attract hummingbirds, who suck their nectar through hollow, "soda-straw" tongues. Not so familiar is the edible fruit that forms after flowering, varying in shape and in color from clear green to bright crimson to dark purple depending on the species or variety.

Cuttings of four to five inches are easily rooted and insure reproduction without variation. (Seeds may introduce unexpected characteristics.) Spring cuttings from new growth without flower buds are ideal and should be placed in pure sand or in a mixture of one part soil, two parts moss peat and three parts sharp sand with plenty of moisture and good drainage. To promote rooting, remove the bottom leaves and cut through the stem with a sharp knife or razor blade at a

FUCHSIA
Fuchsia *species and cultivars*
Deciduous, perennial shrub or
small tree
Height depends on variety
Fast grower
Propagate from cuttings
Sun; light shade in warmer areas
Not hardy; usually needs
winter protection
Fruit eaten
Flowers in summer
Harvest after flowering and
continuous until frost
Various colors

Fuchsia

point just below where a pair of leaves was attached. When cuttings are well rooted, about six weeks, transplant to a four-inch pot with good drainage; keep moist and protect from excessive sun. Plant in a larger container or in the ground when roots protrude through the bottom of the original pot.

Fuchsias prefer semi-shade and can't stand wind. They establish quickly if fed monthly with fish emulsion or similar fertilizer. Winter frost protection is essential.

Some varieties can be grown as ground cover. Others form good-size bushes, or, if kept to a single stalk and staked, miniature trees. A spreading supporting structure at the top of the stake will aid lateral growth at the desired height. Fuchsias in hanging baskets or pots have a lush, tropical appearance.

Pruning should be severe in early spring just as the fuchsia starts to leaf. Cut back at least to wood produced the previous year, even farther if necessary to shape the plant. Dormant buds lie at the base of each leaf ready to spring into action, so recovery is rapid.

Younger plants are susceptible to aphids, white flies, snails, slugs and mildew and should be protected accordingly. Spraying the foliage with water helps disturb the white flies' life cycle and refreshes the plants. Sulphur is effective against mildew. Empty orange or grapefruit halves attract slugs for easy disposal. Otherwise, fuchsias are generally free of pests.

Consult your nurseryman for which of the thousands of varieties now available you'd like best. Colors from purple to red, fuchsia to pink to white are available in overall flower coloring and also in petal variations. Medium-size blossoms generally produce the best fruit for use in the kitchen.

Fuchsia fruit are best when picked one or two days after the fuchsia blossom has withered and fallen. The darker fruit has a more concentrated and pleasant taste than that of a lighter cast. Wash the fruit well, cut off the stem and blossom end and slice. This fruit seems to lend itself best to desserts and dessert sauces. It has a unique flavor and, like rose hips, should be combined with potato flour or corn-flour to temper the slightly astringent taste. For a truly different dessert, surprise your guests with fuchsia pie or small, open tarts.

FUCHSIA CAKE

Combine:
9 ounces flour
1 teaspoon baking powder
7 ounces castor sugar
Cut in:
4 ounces shortening
Add and blend well:
2 eggs, beaten
Pat into 8-inch spring-form tin.
Toss:
about 1 pint sliced fuchsia fruit
2 teaspoons cornflour
1/4 teaspoon cinnamon
1/8 teaspoon freshly grated nutmeg
2 tablespoons castor sugar
Arrange on cake and bake in 375° oven 30 to 40 minutes until edges are brown and fruit is soft. Serve with:
whipped cream flavored with cherry heering

FUCHSIA DESSERT SAUCE

Combine:
4 cups thinly sliced fuchsia fruit
1/4 cup sugar
1 teaspoon arrowroot
1-1/2 tablespoons lemon juice
1/4 teaspoon each allspice and cinnamon
Cover and cook slowly until fruit is very soft. Mash lightly and serve warm or cold over ice cream, pudding or custard.
Makes approximately 2 cups

Geranium

(*Pelargonium* species and cultivars)

GERANIUM
Pelargonium *species and cultivars*
Perennial ground cover, or
suitable for bedding
Normally 2 to 3 feet in height;
up to 5 feet
Fast grower
Propagate from cuttings
Sun
Not hardy; place out after frost
and overwinter indoors
Leaves eaten
Flowers early summer until frost
Light purple and red flowers

Geranium

Originating in South Africa, oak-leaved geraniums were introduced to England in the 17th century and raised as greenhouse plants. During Victorian times, they became a great status symbol as they fit in naturally with gargantuan feasts, plush upholstery and soldiers' red coats. Every suburban villa maintained a staff of jobbing gardeners to care for them in the unfriendly climate. No "proper" garden or hothouse was complete without this good-tempered flower.

Pelargos means "stork"; botanists named geraniums *Pelargonium* after their seed capsule's resemblance to a stork's beak. As geraniums come in such an infinite variety—orange, lime, thyme, spearmint, peppermint, rose, nutmeg, lemon, apple, coconut, filbert, strawberry—it is better when selecting plants for the garden and the kitchen to specify flavor rather than research the many scientific names.

Seeds germinate easily in early spring for subsequent transfer to pots and later bedding out in the garden. To ensure plants identical to the parent, take cuttings of four to six inches in August. Cut through stem just below a leaf junction, remove half the leaves to give a bare stem about three inches long and insert in moist sandy compost. Kept moist, the cuttings should root by early autumn. Transfer to pots over winter, indoors or out depending upon the climate, and transplant in the spring. Keep moist the first few months of growth; when plants are established and start to flower, watering can be cut down.

Geraniums will stand sun and must be protected from slugs and snails. Though they don't require rich soil, they cannot withstand frost and in cold areas must be lifted and wintered in a frost-free location. During this period they will not require much moisture but should not be allowed to dry out completely.

Prune to keep foliage in bounds and remove flowers as they fade to beautify and provide more strength for new blossoms.

Because the leaves of the genus *Pelargonium* are available in a variety of flavors, you should select leaves with a taste and fragrance that will best complement the food to be cooked or garnished. Be cautious when adding geranium leaves. The strength varies with the variety; add gradually and taste as you go. The geranium flower is also edible; experiment, using it like you would other edible flowers.

SERVING HINTS

• Geranium leaves make an excellent garnish for moulded salads, hors d'oeuvre and pâtés.
• Use leaves as a base for holding chopped garnishes or float them artistically in cold drinks.
• Arrange geranium flowers in the bottom of a cake tin before pouring in the batter, or set them on a cake rack, turn out cake onto rack and let it absorb the essence of the flowers while cooling.
• To add flavor to jellies, add leaves to the jar before the hot jelly is poured in.
• Use crushed leaves as a flavoring for soups, poultry, fish, sauces, custards and fruit puddings.

Geranium

RICE PORK BALLS

Combine:
1 pound lean pork, minced
1 egg, beaten
**2 dried wild mushrooms,
 soaked and finely chopped**
**4 tablespoons finely chopped
 water chestnuts**
**2 tablespoons finely chopped
 spring onions**
1 slice ginger root, finely chopped
1 garlic clove, finely chopped
1 teaspoon cornflour
1/2 teaspoon each salt and sugar
**1/4 teaspoon freshly ground
 black pepper**
Fry a small amount to test for
seasonings and adjust. Form into
4 dozen 1-inch balls and
refrigerate.
Boil for 5 minutes, covered:
1/2 pint water
4 or 5 geranium leaves
Remove leaves and add to boiling
water:
**4-1/2 ounces long-grain white rice,
 well washed and drained**

Cover and cook over low heat
about 20 minutes until rice is
fluffy, but still holds together.
Press rice around pork balls to
cover them completely and
refrigerate at least 1 hour.
Place balls, not touching, in pie
dish. Put dish on rack over
boiling water in large pot or
steamer. Cover and steam 15
minutes. Serve as appetizer
sprinkled with:
soy sauce
aji (hot chili-flavored) oil
sake or dry sherry
rice vinegar
Makes 4 dozen balls

CAULIFLOWER IN GERANIUM SAUCE

Crisp in salted ice water to cover:
**1 medium-large head cauliflower
 broken into cauliflowerets**
Sauté, covered, 5 minutes in:
2 tablespoons butter
**3 tablespoons each finely
 chopped onion, carrot and
 celery with leaves**
1 teaspoon finely chopped garlic
Add:
cauliflowerets
5 tablespoons dry white wine
1 tablespoon tomato paste
**1/4 teaspoon each crushed
 coriander seed, salt and freshly
 ground white pepper**
**6 to 8 whole nutmeg geranium
 leaves**
Cover and cook, stirring often,
until cauliflower is just tender,
adding water if too dry. Discard
geranium leaves and adjust seasonings. Serve hot with sauce and:
**generous sprinkling of finely
 chopped parsley**
Or chill and serve as vegetable
appetizer.
Serves 6 as vegetable course,
12 as appetizer

Gladiolus

(*Gladiolus* species and cultivars)

Native to South Africa and the Mediterranean region, this wild plant was named *Gladiolus* or "little sword" by Pliny from the shape of its leaves. Its beauty, not presumed medical or culinary virtues, made it famous. Many claim Christ referred to the gladiolus when he said, "Consider the lilies and how they grow." In 1823 William Colville introduced the first hybrid, *G. colvillei,* a cross between two African species. This opened the floodgates of hybridization and led to extensive garden culture by such diverse horticulturists as Napoleon's gardener at Fontainebleau, Le Moine, Van Houtte and Luther Burbank. All did much to popularize "glads" and build up today's thousands of varieties from the 150 varieties of old.

Gladiolus can easily be grown from seeds or corms (bulb-like stem bases). Loosely called "bulbs," there are actually three under-

GLADIOLUS
Gladiolus *species and cultivars*
Herbaceous, bulbous perennial
To 4 feet in height depending on variety
Propagate from young cormels formed on base of old corm or seed
Sun
Not hardy; overwinter in warmer areas, plant each year in colder areas
Flowers eaten
Flowers summer and early autumn
Various colors

Gladiolus

ground plant structures that produce new growth. True bulbs are underground leaves adapted for storage, like onions. Rhizomes are swollen roots that send up new shoots such as iris. Corms are swollen stems that develop underground such as gladiolus. All can be separated from the mother plant and replanted instead of starting from seeds.

In the case of gladiolus, discard the parent (old) corm and plant back the newly formed corms (diameter of an egg cup). Smaller corms (cormels) should be planted like seeds; they may produce flowers a season earlier than seeds, but not always.

After the plant flowers, remove the gladiolus flower spike and stop watering. When the leaves begin to brown lift all plants unless you live in a warm area and don't care about overcrowding. Leave the tops on and store in a dry, well-ventilated spot until stems are completely brown. Then remove stems and old corms and separate young corms by size for replanting in the spring. Larger bulbs will flower the following summer. Smaller corms and seeds should be planted in narrow shallow drills for lifting in autumn and replanting the next spring in deeper rows to produce "bulb-size" corms for the next year's flowering. The sequence may seem confusing, but actually is fascinating and most rewarding when the colorful flowers bloom. Varied sizes and colors are available to suit different planting areas.

Thrips, which scar the leaves, call for insecticide spray; a basal-plate root rot calls for discarding suspect corms, leaving only the healthy ones to carry on.

Gladiolus should be picked in the early morning before the sun is on them. Wash flowers thoroughly but gently, dry and wrap in paper towels. Place in a plastic bag and refrigerate. They may be crisped in ice water just before using. Although gladiolus petals have only a slight flavor and lose their color when cooked, they add texture and color to salads and if added the last minute, to creamed fish, mashed potatoes, creamed corn, soups, custard, sauces and omelettes. Remove stamens and fill flowers with chicken, tuna, salmon or prawn salad, arrange on a bed of lettuce and garnish with watercress. Or use the flowers, attractively arranged at a buffet, to hold dips. Gladiolus can also be dried (page 27) and crumbled into dishes for flavor and a bit of color.

COLD CORN AND COURGETTE CHOWDER

Cut kernels from:
2 large ears fresh corn
Reserve kernels and cut cobs into several pieces. Set aside.
Sauté until tender but not brown in:
2 tablespoons olive oil
1 small onion, finely chopped
1 teaspoon finely chopped garlic
Add:
cut-up corn cobs
2-1/2 pints lamb stock
4 parsley sprigs
Bring to boil, cook 5 minutes and discard cobs and parsley.
Add:
reserved kernels
Bring back to gentle boil and cook 5 minutes. Add:
6 to 8 courgettes, shredded
Boil gently 3 minutes. Cool and add:
5 tablespoons chopped gladiolus petals
8 fluid ounces double cream
Refrigerate at least 4 hours until very cold. Season with:
salt
freshly ground white pepper
Pour into 6 to 8 chilled bowls and garnish with:
sieved hard-boiled eggs
chopped gladiolus petals
Serves 6 to 8

BEAN SALAD WITH GLADIOLUS

Bring to boil:
1-1/2 pints water
Gradually add and boil 2 minutes:
6 ounces dried haricot or black-eyed beans
Remove from heat and let stand 1 hour. Add and bring back to boil:
1/2 teaspoon salt
bouquet garni of 1 bay leaf, 3 parsley sprigs, 2 onion slices and 1/2 celery stalk and leaves
Cover with lid slightly tilted and boil gently 50 minutes, or until beans are tender but still retain their shape. Drain, discard bouquet garni and set beans aside to cool to room temperature.

To make dressing combine:
6 tablespoons olive oil
2 to 3 tablespoons lemon juice
1 teaspoon Dijon-style mustard (optional)
3 tablespoons finely chopped parsley
2 tablespoons each finely chopped garlic chives and bulbs (page 62)
1 tablespoon finely chopped tarragon (optional)
1 teaspoon finely chopped dill
Toss dressing lightly into beans, cover and refrigerate to blend flavors. Just before serving, toss in:
1 or 2 hard-boiled eggs, chopped
6 to 8 tablespoons chopped gladiolus petals
Mound bean mixture on bed of:
lettuce
Surround with:
tomato wedges
gladiolus blossoms stuffed with a little bean mixture
Decorate top with:
additional chopped gladiolus petals
Serves 6 to 8

Grapevine

(*Vitis vinifera* and cultivars and
Vitis labrusca and cultivars)

The grape family, *Vitaceae,* encompasses such non-fruit-bearing plants as Japanese ivy and Virginia creeper, but their edible cousin, the common grapevine, can be just as decorative. Growing wild in many areas, it produces smaller, sweeter fruit with tougher skin than cultivated varieties.

Grapes have been cultivated for thousands of years. From ancient Persia, *Vitis vinifera* was taken to Egypt, Greece and Sicily, and from that seat of ancient civilization it is said to have spread to Italy, Spain and France. The Romans introduced it to Britain where large vineyards producing good wine were common up to the early 1900's. Bede (the "Venerable Bede"), a monk who wrote England's earliest history circa 720, mentions how wine and honey were turned into mead, the national drink of the time.

Grapes, vines and wine are linked in etymology to *viere,* to twist. Some twisting grapevines live for centuries. Pliny reported one vine being 600 years old, and the great 'Black Hamburg' vine in Hampton Court near London is still producing fruit after two hundred years.

The grapevine thrives best in warm areas, yet is hardy enough to produce well in harsh climates, too. Its tremendous new growth each year so quickly covers arbors and trellises that mature vines often require drastic thinning to prevent overcrowding.

Select a variety suited to local conditions and plant in a sunny location, preferably on a slope where roots can grow deep in well-drained soil. The only required food is nitrogen, in organic form or

GRAPEVINE
Vitis vinifera *and cultivars and* Vitis
labrusca *and cultivars*
Deciduous perennial vine
Height depends on training;
can spread many feet
Fast grower
Propagate from cuttings or eyes
Sun
Hardy, depending on variety
Fruit and leaves eaten
Harvest in late summer and autumn

Grapevine

prepared fertilizer. A few varieties are susceptible to mildew, and leaf hoppers occasionally are a problem. Both should be controlled.

Pruning differs from most climbing plants. After planting and watering well, allow shoots to develop, then reduce them to four or five. As soon as the leaves fall, remove all but the sturdiest cane (sometimes two). Cut this cane back to about three feet, leaving three or four buds. In the second spring prune so as to leave the strongest shoot, allowing two or three branches to form at the desired height. During the summer tip all the young shoots to encourage further branching, cutting them back to one or two buds in the third winter and removing weak and poorly spaced shoots. In the fourth winter prune laterals back to two buds, which should then produce fruit.

Branches and spurs that have borne fruit should be cut back to encourage new fruit-producing laterals. From this point on, prune where necessary to make sure branches are well spaced. With this care the vines will outlive many generations of gardeners.

Grapes are available in such a variety of forms and colors there is no need to restrict either your garden or kitchen to only one kind. Select the vines with the colors and forms of grapes you need—red, white, seedless, thin skinned, early maturing, late maturing, etc. With variety, your garden will be more attractive and the dishes you create more interesting.

There is no better way to eat grapes than fresh picked from the vine; however, they are versatile and can be combined with other foods and served for any course from the appetizer to the dessert. Grapes are excellent added to sauces, served with duck, made into ketchup or jelly.

The leaves of the grapevine are also edible. They can be used as a wrapping for fish, fowl, rice or myriad of other mixtures; quail, poussins or small game birds can be wrapped in the leaves and baked. When picking leaves to use as wrapping, sample as you go. Some leaves may be bitter in which case they should be avoided. It is said that when leaves have a bluish cast on the underside they make especially good eating. Nasturtium leaves may be substituted in recipes calling for grape leaves.

GRAPE LEAVES

Gather leaves in June when full sized but still tender. Blanch 1 minute, drain, dry with paper towels and blanch or brine according to the following method.

To brine: Wash and remove half of stem. Stack 25 to 30 leaves, fold over and tie with string. Bring salted water (1/2 cup salt to 8 cups water) to rolling boil, stirring to dissolve salt. Dip a grape bundle at a time into the boiling brine for 10 seconds. Remove to hot sterilized jars, packing bundles tightly. Cover with brine and seal. Store at least 1 week before using. An alternative method is to layer the leaves, sprinkling each with salt, in a jar or crock. Cover and store in a cool place.

To use: Wash leaves individually, remove tough stem ends and spread out on paper towels shiny side down. Place 1 to 3 tablespoons filling on stem end of leaf, roll swiss-roll fashion, tucking sides in as you roll, and place seam side down in a heavy shallow saucepan. Cook as directed.

STUFFED GRAPE LEAVES

Combine:
1/4 pound rice, cooked
1/2 pound lean minced lamb
4 tablespoons chopped onion
1/2 teaspoon chopped garlic
3 tablespoons chopped parsley
1-1/2 teaspoons chopped oregano
3 tablespoons finely chopped
    pine nuts
1/2 teaspoon salt
1/4 teaspoon freshly ground
    black pepper
6 ounces, peeled, seeded and
    finely chopped tomatoes
Sauté a small amount and adjust
seasonings. Prepare 36 grape
leaves about 3-1/2 inches in
diameter (or 18 large leaves) as
directed in previous recipe. Fill
and roll, place seam side down in
shallow saucepan and fill 1/2 inch
up sides of pan with a mixture of:
beef stock or consommé
2 to 3 teaspoons lemon juice
Place a plate on top to weigh
down, cover, bring to gentle boil
and simmer 15 to 25 minutes
depending upon size. To serve,
remove to heated platter and bind
juices with egg yolk; or add sour
cream. Pour over rolls and garnish
with lemon wedges. Or cool in
juices, remove and pat dry. Serve
cold plain or with sour cream.

CREAM CHEESE AND GRAPE SPREAD

Purée in blender:
3 ounces chopped seeded small
    red dessert grapes
2 ounces cream cheese
Add and blend thoroughly:
2 ounces cream cheese, softened
1/4 teaspoon Worcestershire sauce
1/8 teaspoon freshly ground
    black pepper
Adjust seasonings and refrigerate.
Mound in center of serving
platter. Sprinkle with:
freshly ground black pepper
Surround with:
chopped seeded grapes
Garnish with:
parsley sprigs
Serve with bland crackers.
Makes approximately 15
small servings

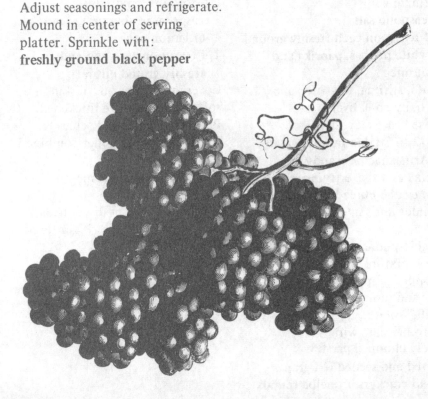

Grapevine

CHICKEN LIVER PÂTÉ

Halve, seed and chop:
4 ounces red dessert grapes
Place in colander to drain.
Sauté 3 minutes in:
**3 tablespoons each butter and
  rendered chicken fat**
1 small onion, finely chopped
1/2 teaspoon finely chopped garlic
Add:
1 pound chicken livers, quartered
Sprinkle with:
1 teaspoon salt
**1/4 teaspoon each freshly ground
  white pepper, paprika and
  nutmeg**
Sauté, stirring, to stiffen and
partially cook livers.
Raise heat and add:
**1-1/2 to 2 tablespoons heated
  Armagnac or brandy**
Flame and shake frying pan until
flames die. Purée liver mixture in
blender until smooth and blend
in:
3 tablespoons softened butter
Cool mixture and stir in reserved
chopped grapes. Adjust seasonings and mound on serving plate.
Chill. When ready to serve
surround pâté with:
finely chopped parsley
halved and seeded red grapes
bland crackers or melba rounds

GRAPE PUDDING

Working over saucepan to catch
juices, peel and halve:
2 pounds black grapes
Reserve skins and cook pulp in
covered saucepan with juices
until seeds loosen. Sieve and
discard seeds. Combine pulp with
skins and:
4 tablespoons sugar
1 tablespoon quick tapioca
2 teaspoons lemon juice
**1 teaspoon freshly grated orange
  or lemon peel**
**1/4 teaspoon each salt and
  freshly grated nutmeg**
Cover and simmer until skins are
soft and juices have thickened.
Purée in blender and set aside.
In top of double boiler combine:
1/2 pint milk
2 tablespoons cornflour
4 tablespoons sugar
Cook and stir over direct heat
until very thick. Whisk a little of
this mixture into:
2 eggs, lightly beaten

Blend into remaining mixture
and place over simmering water.
Cook and stir until again thickened. Blend in puréed grapes,
cool and refrigerate. Just before
serving fold in:
1/4 pint double cream, whipped
Spoon into chilled parfait glasses.
Top each serving with:
2 candied violets (page 30)
Serves 6 to 8

TRIFLE

In large crystal bowl layer:
spongecake
Pour over to saturate:
sherry, rum or brandy
Sprinkle with:
3 ounces toasted slivered almonds
Refrigerate. Just before serving
pour grape pudding (preceding
recipe) over. Whip until just
barely stiff:
1/4 pint double cream
1/2 tablespoon icing sugar
Add:
1/2 teaspoon vanilla essence or
1 teaspoon rose water
Pile on top of pudding and serve
immediately, garnished with:
candied violets (page 30)
Serves 8 to 10

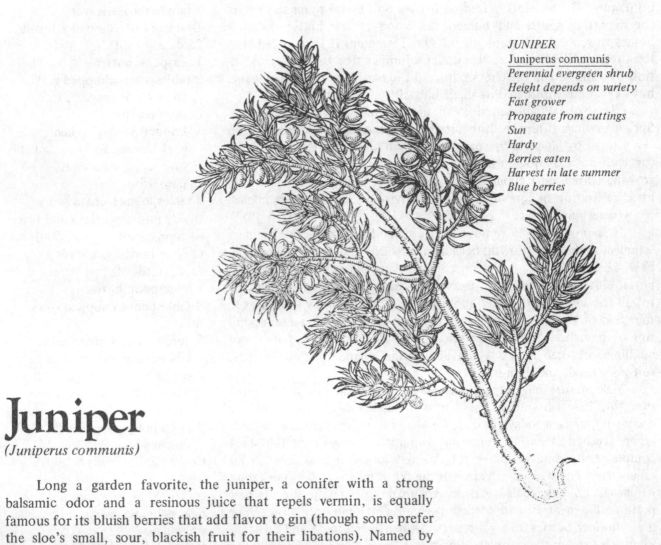

JUNIPER
Juniperus communis
Perennial evergreen shrub
Height depends on variety
Fast grower
Propagate from cuttings
Sun
Hardy
Berries eaten
Harvest in late summer
Blue berries

Juniper
(Juniperus communis)

Long a garden favorite, the juniper, a conifer with a strong balsamic odor and a resinous juice that repels vermin, is equally famous for its bluish berries that add flavor to gin (though some prefer the sloe's small, sour, blackish fruit for their libations). Named by Virgil and Pliny in the Mediterranean area, the juniper's true origin

Juniper

is a mystery, for it appears to be native to many other parts of the world. Perhaps its durable seeds, which could survive prolonged storage during slow sea voyages, offer an explanation for its ubiquity.

In history, the juniper has generally been used to ward off evil influences. The ancients placed its berries on funeral pyres to protect the departing spirit, and burned the wood of the juniper in their homes to repel the demons. In the Old Testament it is recorded that the prophet Elijah took refuge under a juniper tree to avoid persecution by King Ahab. The Greeks thought the berries of medicinal value, but like Virgil, considered its shade unhealthy.

Seeds sown a half-inch deep in the autumn germinate in spring. Spring sowings often lie dormant through the summer. Propagation can also be by layers or by spring cuttings in sandy soil exposed to the sun with both adequate drainage and moisture. Most varieties are low growing (three feet), though a few become 40-foot trees. They require little cultivation or care and can even survive weed-control chemicals. No wonder junipers are so popular!

It is important to remove all weeds and grasses before junipers establish their dense growth, because afterwards it's almost impossible. Few diseases attack, but sprays may be needed to combat the tip borer, either as a preventive measure in the spring or as an insecticide to kill the moths when they appear and are about to lay their eggs in the stem of the plants. The hatching larvae bore around stems and kill tips of branches. Nurserymen select desirable forms from batches of seedlings and can advise which outstanding characteristics will best suit your needs and desires.

Pick mature blue juniper berries and let them dry slowly until they turn blackish and are ready to use. Like Douglas fir tips, juniper berries impart a woodsy flavor to foods with which they are cooked. When crushed, they discharge an aromatic, astringent oil that best complements game or other full-flavored foods such as cabbage or sauerkraut. The berries will also cut the fat of meats such as pork, and if placed on the coals when barbecuing, will purify the air and perfume the meat. For an interesting change, make juniper olive oil, or mash juniper berries into your next terrine. In Scotland and Sweden, juniper is used in the smoking of hams.

110

CABBAGE ROLLS

Cook for 3 minutes in boiling salted water:

8 large cabbage leaves

Drain and dry on paper towels. Sauté until soft in:

1 teaspoon butter

2 tablespoons chopped garlic chive bulbs (page 62)

Combine with:

3/4 pound well-seasoned pork sausage meat (or substitute venison sausage, page 158)

4 tablespoons tomato sauce

Divide into 8 portions and place each on a cabbage leaf. Roll, tucking in edges, and set aside. Sauté until soft in:

1 tablespoon butter

4 tablespoons chopped onion

Add:

6 fluid ounces tomato sauce

4 tablespoons rich beef stock

Place rolls seam side down in mixture and tuck in between rolls:

8 to 10 juniper berries, lightly crushed

Cover tightly, bring to gentle boil, lower heat and simmer gently 20 minutes or until cabbage is tender. Serve with the sauce.

Serves 4

JUNIPER BERRY
BUTTER SAUCE

Add and cook until soft in:
4 tablespoons melted butter
3 tablespoons finely chopped onion
1 teaspoon finely chopped garlic
Remove from heat and add:
3 to 4 juniper berries, lightly
    crushed
2 to 3 teaspoons lemon juice
1 tablespoon chopped parsley
salt and freshly ground white
    pepper to taste
Serve on baked potatoes with
sprinkling of chives and parsley,
asparagus or vegetable spaghetti
(following recipe).
Makes 4 to 6 tablespoons

STEAMED
VEGETABLE SPAGHETTI

Halve and scoop out seeds from:
1 1-1/2-pound vegetable spaghetti
Place halves skin side down in
steamer and dot with:
3 tablespoons butter
Sprinkle with:
1/2 teaspoon salt
1/4 teaspoon each freshly ground
    white pepper and powdered
    oregano

Cover and steam 35 to 40 minutes or until tender. With fork,
remove flesh and place "spaghetti"
strands in heated serving dish.
Pour juniper berry butter sauce
over and serve immediately. Also
good with any tomato and/or
spaghetti meat sauce.
Serves 6 to 8

MASHED POTATOES
WITH CABBAGE

Sauté until soft in:
4 tablespoons butter
4 tablespoons each finely
    chopped onion and celery
    stalks with leaves
Add:
8 ounces finely shredded cabbage
4 juniper berries, lightly crushed
4 tablespoons rich beef stock
Cover and cook until cabbage
is wilted and just tender. Add to:
1-1/2 pounds hot mashed potatoes
Season to taste with:
salt
freshly ground black pepper
cayenne pepper
Serves 8

VENISON FONDUE

Cut into 3/4-inch cubes:
2 pounds tender cut of venison
In fondue pot or electric frying
pan combine:
3/4 pint corn oil
8 ounces clarified butter
2 thyme sprigs
Keeping fat at 375°, dip meat
cubes into fat until done to taste.
Serve with juniper berry sauce
(see preceding) as a dip. Good
with baked potatoes and coconut
beans (page 45).
Serves 4 to 6

Lavender
(Lavandula vera)

LAVENDER
Lavandula vera
Perennial shrub
3 to 5 feet in height
Fast grower
Propagate from cuttings
Sun
Not fully hardy; may need
winter protection
Leaves eaten
Flowers in summer
Blue flowers

Another Mediterranean original, lavender (from *lavare,* to wash) has made its biggest contribution in the scented cosmetics field. Ingested as tea or applied externally as an oil, poultice, water or fomentation, lavender was ascribed powers to alleviate or cure such diverse maladies as "bitings of serpents; hysterick fits; distempers of the head, womb, or stomach; vertigo; barrenness of women; aching joints and headaches from fatigue and exhaustion; bruises, cuts and bites; lice on animals." Some books warned that the excessive use of lavender oil or essence of lavender could be harmful. Others attest to the fragrance's ability to make lions and tigers docile. Truly remarkable is this plant with its long spikes of fragrant, pale purple flowers and contrasting greyish foliage, so well known for use in sachets.

Almost forgotten is lavender's use as a condiment for flavoring various dishes, and even these were described in old times as a "comfort for the stomach." Most of the medicinal claims are in limbo, but lavender's delicate fragrance and pronounced flavor in the kitchen deserve to be rediscovered.

The lavender's 20-odd species include the commercially grown *L. vera* and *L. spica,* which even botanists have difficulty distinguishing. Light, well-drained loam is best for growing, since lavender is susceptible to winter rot in wet ground. While not too hardy, it will withstand some frost and will sprout from the base if cut back. Propagate with cuttings taken in summer, rooted in sandy soil and lightly protected. or with firmer cuttings in September/October, which can be rooted out of doors. Cut back in March when too leggy, and allow new growth to take over. Replant every five years or so.

Honey fungus and caterpillars may attack, but seldom present serious threats. In July and August flowers should be promptly harvested before rains cause them to deteriorate.

Use leaves that are three to four inches long. Wash thoroughly but gently and pat dry. The flowers and leaves may be used fresh or dried for winter use. The flavor and fragrance of lavender are pervasive so it must always be added with a cautious hand. However, there are many uses for this most versatile herb in the kitchen.

SERVING HINTS

• Use the flowers alone or a small sprig as a garnish for martinis or fruit punches.

• Dried or fresh, the flowers make a fragrant, and some say healthful, tea.

• Chop the flowers and leaves into salads (such as raw vegetable with chives), dressings, fruit desserts or sprinkle them over pineapple marinated in kirsch.

• Add lavender sprigs to beef stew, pork roast or lamb, or place a sprig or two in the oven when roasting chicken.

• Infuse honey, vinegar or sugar with fresh lavender.

• Place petals or sprigs in the bottom of the jar before pouring in hot lavender jelly. Serve the jelly with cold lamb.

• An English favorite is salad served on a bed of lettuce and lavender sprigs. And it is recorded that Queen Elizabeth I was particularly fond of lavender conserve; try making one with mixed fruit, nuts and brown sugar.

• Fresh lavender can be candied or pickled.

Lavender

SPICED ORANGES

Combine:
1/4 pint water
6 tablespoons sugar
8 fluid ounces red wine
4 slices lemon
4 whole cloves
1 4-inch stick cinnamon
12 1-inch lavender leaves
Bring to boil, reduce heat and
simmer, stirring occasionally until
syrupy. Place in crystal bowl:
6 oranges, segmented
Strain syrup over and chill
3 hours or more. Garnish with:
mint sprigs
Serve for brunch or as dessert.
Serves 8

SHELLFISH SOUP

Sauté until soft in:

3 tablespoons olive oil
5 ounces chopped onion
1 teaspoon finely chopped garlic
Push onion aside and sauté
quickly:
3 to 4 ounces diced ham
1/2 pound raw prawns, cleaned
4 tablespoons ground blanched
   almonds
Stir constantly and cook until
prawns just turn pink.
Remove prawns and reserve.
Add to ham mixture and cook
for 15 minutes:
4 pints lavender beef stock
   (page 28)
Bring stock to boil and stir in:
6 ounces raw rice, well washed
Cook 20 minutes until rice is
almost tender. Raise heat and
add:
5 ounced fresh peas
2 pints clams or mussels
Cook just until clams or mussels
open, add prawns and reheat.
Adjust seasonings with:
salt and black pepper

Ladle soup into tureen or large
individual bowls, making sure
each bowl has ham, prawns and
clams or mussels. Sprinkle with:
2 hard-boiled eggs, chopped
coriander or parsley
Pass a bowl of finely chopped
garlic and a peppermill and serve
with French bread and salad.
Serves 6 to 8 as main meal

WON TON ROLLS

Cook, covered, until chicken is
tender:
1 tablespoon each soy sauce
   and butter
1 slice ginger root
1 garlic clove
2 tablespoons sake or dry sherry
1 chicken breast
Cool and finely chop the
chicken. Strain and measure
cooking liquid and add to it to
make 1/2 pint:
chicken stock
Sauté until soft in:
2 tablespoons butter
4 tablespoons each finely chopped
   celery and onion
1/2 teaspoon very finely chopped
   lavender

Add chicken and chicken
stock. Cook until all moisture is
gone and blend in:
2 teaspoons cornflour
salt, pepper and nutmeg to taste
Cool and blend in:
1 large egg, beaten
Have ready:
48 won ton skins*
Working with 6 skins at a time
and keeping rest covered, place
about 1 teaspoon filling on lower
edge, 1/2 inch from edges. Roll
like a cigar and seal upper edge
with water. Place seam side down
on baking sheet. Keep covered
with tea towel. Repeat, making
48 cigars in all. Remove towel,
cover securely with self-sealing
wrap and refrigerate until ready
to serve. Deep fry until just
golden, drain on paper towels
and serve immediately with dip
of:
soy sauce
sake
finely chopped ginger root and
   garlic (optional)
Makes 48

* Available in many Chinese provision stores.

Lavender Cotton
(Santolina chamaecyparissus)

LAVENDER COTTON
Santolina chamaecyparissus
Perennial, low shrub ground cover
1 to 2 feet in height
Slow grower
Propagate from cuttings
Sun
Hardy except in very cold areas
Foliage eaten
Flowers in summer
Harvest year round
Yellow flowers,
white-silvery foliage

While most garden plants were first cultivated for medicinal or culinary purposes, the lavender cotton, one of the finest white- or silver-leaved dwarf shrubs, was evidently domesticated for decorative purposes only. It prefers well-drained, sunny slopes, poor to semi-rich soil and is capable of standing drought—in other words, it thrives under conditions like those of its native Southern Europe. That an attractive plant so easily grown has not enjoyed wider enthusiasm is surprising.

A woody, evergreen perennial herb with yellow flowers, lavender cotton roots easily when early summer cuttings (no longer than four to six inches) are placed in a sandy mixture and shielded from the sun for a few days. Rooted branches from established plants can also sometimes be separated for replanting.

Cultivation is minimal. Pruning consists of shearing back in the spring or early autumn when the plant gets leggy. Slugs and snails should be treated if they attack the young growth, but otherwise lavender cotton is essentially pest free.

Lavender cotton has been long admired primarily for its decorative appeal and use as an air freshener. However, its pleasant fragrance, released when the shoots are crushed, makes it a natural addition to the kitchen.

SERVING HINTS

- Sprigs of lavender cotton will add flavor to a pork roast or other cooked meats.
- Infuse beef stock with lavender cotton sprigs.
- Prepare a fresh tomato sauce with minced turkey
and lavender cotton sprigs. During the last few minutes of cooking time, remove the sprigs and add chopped courgettes, simmering just until tender. Serve over fresh noodles.

BULGHUR PILAF

Sauté until golden in:
3 tablespoons butter
8 ounces bulghur (cracked wheat)
6 to 8 tablespoons finely chopped onion
1 teaspoon finely chopped fresh oregano or marjoram
Add:
1-1/4 pints lavender cotton beef stock (page 28)
1/2 teaspoon salt
1/4 teaspoon freshly ground black pepper
Bring to gentle boil, cover and cook over medium low heat 15 minutes or until bulghur is fluffy and liquid is absorbed. Toss in:
4 tablespoons finely chopped parsley
Transfer to heated serving dish and sprinkle with:
finely chopped chives
paprika
Serves 6

Lavender Cotton

SCALLOPS

Toss and marinate 20 minutes in:
2 tablespoons lemon juice
1-1/2 pounds scallops, halved or
    quartered if large
Bring to boil and simmer
10 minutes:
1/2 pint dry white wine
1/4 pint fish stock or water
1 small onion, sliced
3 parsley sprigs
2 or 3 lavender cotton sprigs
4 peppercorns, crushed
1/4 teaspoon salt if using water
    instead of fish stock
Bring to hard boil and add:
scallops
Cook 3 minutes and strain,
reserving liquid. Remove scallops,
slice and set aside.
Lightly brown in:
2 ounces butter
1/2 pound mushrooms, sliced
1 small onion, chopped
Add and cook 10 minutes:
3 large ripe tomatoes, peeled,
    seeded and chopped
4 tablespoons chopped parsley
dash cayenne pepper
Melt until bubbly:
2 tablespoons butter
Sprinkle with:
2 tablespoons flour

Cook and stir 3 minutes and
then gradually add:
1/2 pint reserved liquid
Cook and stir until thickened.
Combine with tomato mixture
and add:
scallops
2 to 4 tablespoons double cream
salt, freshly ground white pepper
    and lemon juice to taste
Transfer to 6 lightly buttered
ramekins and sprinkle with:
scant 1-1/2 ounces fine bread
    crumbs
paprika
Dot with:
2 tablespoons butter
Bake in 400° oven until bubbly
and slightly browned.
Serves 6

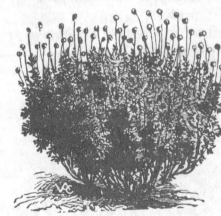

ROAST PORK FILLET

Combine:
3/4 pint grated onion
3 garlic cloves, mashed or finely
    chopped
juice and pulp of 1 large orange
juice and pulp of 1 lemon or lime
3 to 4 sprigs lavender cotton
Add and coat well:
1 pork fillet (about
    1-1/2 pounds)
Turning often, marinate 6 hours.
Scrape off marinade and brown
pork on all sides in:
4 tablespoons butter
Transfer to baking tin and
deglaze frying pan with:
2 tablespoons each dry white
    wine and water
Pour over pork; lay on top:
3 lavender cotton sprigs
Bake in 325° oven, basting often
and adding more wine and/or
water if needed, 1 hour or until
done. Discard lavender cotton
sprigs and transfer to heated
platter and to pan juices blend in:
1/4 pint creamy milk
Heat and pour over roast.
Serves 4 to 6

Lily

(*Lilium* species and varieties)

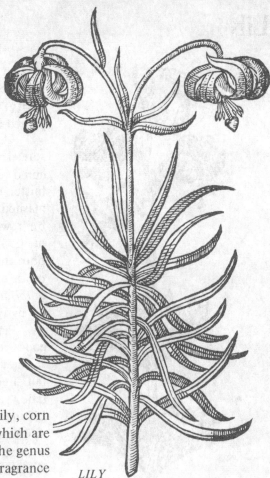

So-called "lilies" include many flowers such as the calla lily, corn lily, day lily, lily of the valley and lily of the Nile, none of which are "true lilies" and some of which are not edible. All flowers of the genus *Lilium*, however, are edible. Their beauty is varied, their fragrance superb, their place in history secure, their culinary uses many.

The Madonna lily *(L. candidum)* was depicted on Cretan vases in 1750 B.C. as a sacred flower of Britomartis, the Minoan goddess of fishermen, hunters and sailors. Greek mythology later embellished its status with the story that Zeus ordered Somnus to give his wife Hera a sleeping draught because she objected to his half-mortal baby son, Hercules. When Hera slept Zeus placed his son at her breast. Hercules sucked so lustily the milk flowed too fast for him to swallow. Some drops remained in the heavens to form the Milky Way, others fell to earth to become Madonna lilies. Aphrodite, out of jealousy, put a large pistil in the mouth of the flower in an attempt to destroy its beauty as compared to the rose.

LILY
Lilium *species and varieties*
Herbaceous, bulbous perennial
6 to 8 feet in height
Fast growing in summer
and spring
Propagate from seed,
scales or offsets
Light shade; shade in
warmer areas
Hardy
Flowers eaten
Flowers in summer,
depending on variety
Various colors

119

Lily

In a more ethereal approach Christians associated the lily with the Madonna because of its colors—white for goodness, gold for purity. Perhaps the lily's elusive fragrance, impossible to preserve, also played a part in its gilded history.

On a more mundane level, one theory conjectures lily culture spread when Roman warriors took plants with them because lily bulbs cured corns. Later medicine prescribed lily and yarrow boiled in butter for smearing on burns. Bulbs were "good to break a boil," and mashed bulb poultices supposedly cured all sorts of ailments. "Lily bulb with honey gleweth together sinuses cut asunder," one early medico claimed. The Chinese, always alert to food possibilities, found both the tiger lily *(L. tigrinum)* flowers and bulbs useful—flowers fresh or dried for seasoning; bulbs for pickling. The Chinese also ate *L. bulbifarum* bulbs and the Japanese the sweet bulbs of *L. auratum.* Bulbs of many other lily species have been eaten locally.

Plant plump lily bulbs in spring or early autumn in soil rich in good humus, that will not become waterlogged. If covered with twice the height of the bulb, plants should not need staking as they grow tall. Feed in the spring with a general garden fertilizer. After blooms fade, remove flower head only, cutting stems later when they die. Lifting and dividing bulbs (discarding tiny ones), and replanting, need not be done until the plants show definite signs of failing, the result of overcrowding. Lilies are easily grown in containers with good drainage if planted deeply. Keep in mind they like their feet in the shade and their heads in the sun.

Tiger lilies have been eaten in the Orient for centuries and, along with day lilies, are more commonly used in cooking than the more recently developed hybrids like 'Bellingham Hybrids,' which may be used in many of the same ways, however; fresh or dried their delicate flavor and fragrance are a delightful addition to many kinds of dishes. Pick the blossoms before the sun is on them, wash thoroughly and pat dry. Unlike the more commonly eaten lilies, the entire flower can be chopped without having to remove the stamen and pistil. Remember not to overcook lilies, as they will lose their texture and flavor.

Lily

SERVING HINTS

• Add fresh lily buds to clear chicken soup during the last 3 minutes of cooking time.
• Add chopped flowers to fruit cake along with jujubes, litchi nuts, almonds, etc.
• Add chopped flowers to egg dishes and salads for a touch of color and hint of sweet taste.
• Steep lily flowers in honey for 1 week.
• Add 1 ounce of dried flowers to 3/4 pint of vinegar.

CURRIED BROWN RICE WITH LILY FLOWERS

Sauté until soft in:
2 tablespoons corn oil
4 ounces onion, thinly sliced
Add:
6 to 8 tablespoons chopped lily flowers
1 garlic clove, finely chopped
2 to 3 slices ginger root, finely chopped
Cook and stir 5 minutes. Add:
8 ounces diced cooked ham
6 ounces brown rice, cooked
1 teaspoon curry powder
salt and pepper to taste
3 to 4 tablespoons stock, if needed for moisture

Sauté until transparent in:
2 tablespoons olive oil
4 ounces onion, thinly sliced
Remove onions with slotted spoon and keep warm.
In same pan sauté:
3 ounces raisins, plumped in 4 tablespoons hot water and drained
Remove raisins and keep warm. Then sauté:
3 to 4 ounces slivered almonds
Turn rice mixture onto heated platter and make well in center. Fill with the onions and surround rice with raisins and almonds. Serve with tomato and green bean salad dressed with oil and vinegar.
Serves 6

POTATO OMELETTE

Scrub but do not peel:
2 new white potatoes, about 6 ounces each
Quarter lengthwise and slice thinly crosswise to make small pieces. Combine with:
4 ounces finely chopped onions
In a frying pan heat:
2 tablespoons garlic olive oil

Add potato mixture. Cover and cook, stirring occasionally, 10 to 15 minutes until potatoes are soft but not browned. Remove from heat and cool 3 minutes. While still warm combine thoroughly with:
2 eggs, beaten
4 tablespoons finely chopped lily petals
Let stand 30 minutes, stirring occasionally. Then heat in a 10-inch frying pan:
1 tablespoon garlic olive oil
Pour in potato mixture and form a cake. Cover and cook over low heat, re-forming cake if necessary, 10 minutes or until eggs are set and bottom is just starting to brown. Carefully remove to plate, and flip omelette over on to another plate. Slid omelette back into pan, adding more oil if needed. Cover and cook over low heat 10 minutes or until starting to brown. Transfer to serving plate and sprinkle with:
2 tablespoons finely chopped lily petals
finely chopped parsley
Cut into wedges. Omelette should be firm but not dry. Serve warm, not hot.

Mulberry

(Morus nigra)

The mulberry tree is truly fabulous, not only because of its history, but also for its multiplicity of uses. Pliny maintained the mulberry was the wisest of all trees, for it waits until after the cold weather, then puts forth buds "in one night and with so much force that their breaking forth may be evidently heard." In Ovid's dramatic myth, the mulberry's fruit was originally white, but became permanently stained when Pyramus fell dying from love's despair on his own sword under mulberry boughs, and his lover later added her blood to the roots. The mulberry is mentioned in the Old Testament: in Samuel and the Psalms. One venerable tree still in existence in England reputedly dates back to 1548 when mulberry trees were imported from Lyon. Shakespeare planted a mulberry tree in 1609 at Stratford that still survives.

The historical cultivation of silkworms on mulberry leaves is probably even more dramatic than that of mulberry fruit. In England in the 1600's, James I offered packets of mulberry tree seeds to all those who would sow them, and the trees became as fashionable as the silk they helped produce. In the Orient, where the mulberry tree is a native plant, it is planted near the water. The silkworms feed on the leaves and fish in the nearby water, in turn, feed on the worms. The fruit is considered a delicacy and the wood, hard and durable, is used for artifacts.

The leaves and branches of a mulberry tree give it an unusual decorative character. Though it may reach heights of up to 30 feet, its round crown is often wider and together with its broad leaves provides excellent shade. It can be espaliered or trained to grow with three- to six-foot trunks before branching (standard or half standard) so its ultimate height can be tailored at will. It is a hardy tree, though it may succumb to prolonged, unusually severe winters. One tree can supply a large family with fruit.

Propagation is simple. After leaves fall take eight-inch cuttings from strong, new growth and place in moistened sandy soil. After rooting occurs in early spring, plant in the garden, then in autumn move to a permanent sunny location with well-drained soil. Trees should be pruned for size, shape and maximum shade. If aphids attack, spray carefully so as not to contaminate the fruit. The white and red mulberries can also be cultivated readily.

Attractive to birds and chipmunks, the mulberry is especially troublesome and messy once the mature dark-colored fruit start to fall. To avoid a clean-up problem, spread a plastic sheet beneath the tree and shake the limbs to release the ripe berries; then gather them carefully from the sheet.

MULBERRY
Morus nigra
Deciduous tree
20 to 30 feet in height
Fast grower
Propagate from cuttings or
buy grafted plants
Sun
Hardy
Berries eaten
Harvest in late summer
Deep red fruit

Mulberry

SERVING HINTS

In the Far East, mulberries are gathered, dried on rooftops in the sun and then stored for winter use.

• Mulberries are good eaten fresh from the tree; plain or dressed with custard sauce.

• Add to pear and cream cheese salad or combine with sour cream dressing for coleslaw.

• Cook mulberries in a pie, alone or with complementary fruit, in compotes, puddings and tarts, and in most ways in which blackberries are cooked.

• Stew fresh berries with sugar and lemon juice to taste as a sauce for serving over ice cream.

• Cook berries down into a juice, jelly or jam.

STEAMED MULBERRY PUDDING

Cream until smooth:
1/4 pound butter
1/4 pound castor sugar
Beat in:
1 beaten egg
Sift together:
7 ounces unbleached flour
1/2 teaspoon baking soda
1/4 teaspoon nutmeg
1/8 teaspoon salt
Add to butter mixture alternately with:
4 tablespoons buttermilk
Then add:
2 tablespoons flour
Batter should be firm but sticky. With floured hands line a buttered 1-1/2-pint pudding basin with pastry; reserve enough to cover top. Fill with:
about 1 pint mulberries
Top with rest of pastry and smooth with spatula. Cover tightly with heavy foil and place on rack in pan with water halfway up sides of basin; cover and steam 3 hours. * Do not let water boil hard; steam should just be escaping. Remove foil and loosen edges of cake with thin knife. Turn out on to serving plate

Cool 3 minutes and slice, letting juices run out. Serve with:
double cream
Or top with:
whipped cream flavored with liqueur of choice
May also be eaten at room temperature.
Serves 8

* A large asparagus steamer works well. Tie a "hammock" around the basin for easy removal.

MULBERRY ZABAGLIONE

In a large, flat-bottom stainless-steel or copper bowl set over steam, beat until frothy:
4 egg yolks
2 tablespoons castor sugar
8 tablespoons Marsala
2 tablespoons dry sherry
Continue beating until thick enough to coat a wooden spoon. Remove from heat and quickly stir in:
1/2 pint mulberries
Serve immediately in stem glasses or glass bowls.
Serves 3 or 4

Nasturtium

(*Tropaeolum majus* and cultivars)

A native of Peru, the nasturtium was introduced in Europe in 1686. Originally admired for its attractive flowers and easy growth, it was later that its culinary applications were explored and the flowers, leaves and seedpods were all found to be edible and flavorful. This common flower was given its Latin name by the great Swedish botanist Carolus Linnaeus (Carl von Linné) in the late 1700's. His classification and naming of plants helped bring order out of botanical chaos by assigning Latin names that are universally recognized, though sometimes confused with common names. For example, if you mention nasturtium to a botanist he might think of the water-cress genus *Nasturtium*. Our nasturtium scientifically bears a more exciting name. Because gardeners often grew nasturtiums on poles, Linnaeus likened their predominate yellow and red flowers to the gold, blood-stained helmets (*tropae*–trophies) of defeated warriors hung on poles in the Roman tradition, hence *Tropaeolum*.

Nasturtium seeds can be sown in the spring in any soil, in partial shade or sun. They tend to become invasive unless trained up wires to form a pyramid of color through the summer. Since snails and slugs love nasturtium foliage of all varieties as much as you will, it behoves you to take appropriate protective measures.

The subtle peppery taste of the nasturtium plant is familiar to gardeners and cooks alike. The flowers, leaves and seedpods are all edible and nutritional, being high in vitamin C. The nasturtium is also said to have an herbal penicillin content which aids in warding off infections. Pick the flowers when fully open but still fresh; they make an attractive garnish for soups and puréed vegetables. The cresslike, mild flavor of the leaves combines well with many foods. The seedpods should be picked when tiny and green just after the flower has withered; when pickled, they make an excellent substitute for capers and are good added to martinis.

NASTURTIUM
Tropaeolum majus and cultivars
Self-seeding annual ground cover
Fast grower
Propagate from seed in spring after frost
Sun or light shade
Leaves, flowers and seedpods eaten
Flowers in summer
Harvest in spring and summer
Red, yellow and orange flowers

Nasturtium

SERVING HINTS

- Fill flowers with a salad or a cream cheese-pineapple mixture to accompany an hors d'oeuvre tray.
- Chop seeds and/or flowers into raw salads for texture, taste and color.
- Mix chopped leaves into a bean and spring onion salad or a cabbage salad with sorrel and caraway seeds.
- Add chopped leaves to salad of tomatoes, cheese, chives and parsley, or to a plate of cucumbers dressed with dill and chives.
- Sprinkle chopped leaves on cold cream soups or combine with chives in an omelette.
- Make a chiffonade with chopped leaves and flowers for a vegetable soup or a fennel salad with dill and poppy seeds.
- Blanch the leaves and use in place of grape leaves when making stuffed grape-leaf recipes.
- Add pickled seedpods to browned butter, blue cheese and lemon juice and serve over cooked vegetables.
- For an unusual salad, combine beetroots, apples, sorrel and nasturtium leaves and pickled seedpods.

PICKLED NASTURTIUM SEEDPODS OR SEEDS

Changing water every day, soak for 3 days in salted water:
nasturtium seedpods or seeds
Drain, dry and layer in jar with:
chopped tarragon
finely chopped onion
Boil 10 minutes:
3/4 pint white wine vinegar
12 peppercorns
1 blade mace
1 teaspoon salt
1/4 teaspoon crushed dried red pepper
1/8 teaspoon nutmeg
Cool, strain and pour over seedpods or seeds. Cover and let stand in refrigerator 1 week before using.

NASTURTIUM-MUSHROOM BAKE

Blanch 30 seconds in salted water:
20 to 30 large nasturtium leaves
Drain leaves and coat with:
garlic olive oil
Have ready:
1/2 pound mushrooms, sliced
Sprinkle mushrooms lightly with:
salt and white pepper
finely chopped thyme

Place one-third of the nasturtium leaves on the bottom of a shallow 6-inch baking dish. Place one-half of the mushrooms on the leaves and repeat layering, ending with the leaves. Sprinkle over top:
garlic olive oil
Cover tightly and bake in a 350° oven 20 minutes or until mushrooms are just tender. Serve with toast fingers.
Serves 4 to 6 as a first course

NASTURTIUM LEAF ROLL-UPS

Blanch for 30 seconds:
nasturtium leaves
Brush both sides lightly with:
olive oil
Place on each leaf:
2 to 3 teaspoons chicken, turkey, ham, tuna or salmon salad
Roll like Swiss roll, tucking in sides, and place seam side down on serving plate. Garnish with:
parsley sprigs
nasturtium flowers stuffed with mixture of softened cream cheese, cream, lemon juice and chopped chives
Serve with mixture of:
mayonnaise
whipped cream

PARSLEY
Petroselinum crispum *and cultivars*
Perennial ground cover; treat
as annual in colder areas
8 to 12 inches in height
Fast grower
Propagate from seed
Sun; light shade in warmer areas
Foliage eaten
Harvest in late spring and summer
White flowers

Parsley

(*Petroselinum crispum* and cultivars)

Carrots, parsnips, celery and parsley are all *Umbelliferae* (plants with a number of flower stalks spreading from a common center to form an "umbrella"). Celery, called the marsh selinon, and parsley, the rock (petro) selinon, are even more closely related, but are quite different in appearance and culinary use.

Ancient Greeks dedicated parsley to Persephone, the queen of Hades and personification of spring, when she was allowed to return to the earth's surface. It played an important role in funeral rites, and because of this, superstitions existed about transplanting young plants. Victors were crowned at the Isthmian games with chaplets of parsley, and, according to Homer, chariot warriors fed parsley to their horses.

Parsley has been credited with curing sick fish when thrown in fish ponds. Charlemagne advocated growing it for medicinal purposes, presumably used in the form of a tea steeped from its dried leaves and roots. Apiol, an oil extracted from its seeds, has been used to treat

Parsley

malaria, and parsley seeds supposedly overcome the odor of garlic. Gerard, in his herbal, claimed its roots or seeds boiled in ale "cast forth strong venome or poyson." What a surprising history for so well-known a plant!

Presumably introduced in Britain about 1550 from Sardinia, parsley thrived in the wild as well as in cultivated gardens. Its feathery foliage now gives pleasure and adds beauty everywhere it grows and to every dish it garnishes.

Parsley is easily raised from seeds, though germination may take as long as eight weeks. Plain-leaved varieties (Italian parsley) are hardier than those with curly leaves and can withstand severe frost. Sowings in early spring, spring, summer and mid-summer assure a continuous supply of fresh sprigs. Sow in drills about half an inch deep as a border for easy cutting, and thin out to eight inches when established. Parsley likes well-worked soil, partial shade and lots of moisture. Keep the surface soil loose and if plants get too tall cut back to the ground, then fertilize and give extra water. Snail and slug bait may be required to protect young growth. If mildew becomes a problem, the plants are not in an airy enough site.

High in vitamins A and C and in iron, parsley is one of the most versatile of all herbs. It combines well with most other herbs and will add flavor and color to a variety of dishes. When chopping, include some of the tender stems, for they contain the most concentrated flavor. Save tough stems for soup stocks or to flavor sauces. The flat variety (Italian parsley) has more intense flavor, while the curly-leafed parsley is more attractive for garnishing. Parsley very quickly deep fried in clarified butter and/or vegetable oil is a superb vegetable by itself.

The root of Hamburg or turnip-rooted parsley can be used like celeriac to flavor soups and stews, or can be cooked like carrots or turnips to accompany stews. The flavor is similar to celeriac and it was considered a delicacy in Victorian England where it was most commonly known as parsnip-rooted parsley. Cook just until tender in salted water or stock. Make a cream sauce with some of the cooking water, bind with egg yolk and season with lemon juice, salt and pepper. Slice the cooked root, combine with cream sauce and garnish with croûtons and parsley.

PARSLEY SAUCE

Melt until bubbly:
2 tablespoons butter
Sprinkle with:
2 tablespoons flour
Cook and stir 3 minutes and
gradually add:
**1/2 pint milk, top of the milk or
stock or water in which
vegetables have been cooked,
or herb or flower stock
(page 28)**
Cook and stir until smooth and
thickened. Continue cooking,
stirring often, 10 minutes. Just
before serving add:
**3 tablespoons or more finely
chopped parsley**
1 tablespoon butter cut in bits
Makes 1/2 pint

CREAM OF PARSLEY SOUP

Sauté until soft and starting to
turn golden in:
2 tablespoons butter
5 ounces onions, chopped
Add:
**1 pound new white potatoes,
scrubbed but skin left on, and
thickly sliced**
1-1/2 pints rich chicken stock
**8 ounces tightly packed chopped
parsley with some stems**
Cover, bring to gentle boil and
cook 15 minutes or until potatoes
are soft. Purée and reheat. Add:
1 tablespoon soy sauce
1/2 tablespoon fresh lemon juice
salt and white pepper to taste
Adjust seasonings, ladle into
heated soup bowls and garnish
with:
lemon slices
finely chopped parsley
paprika
Serves 4 to 6

CELERY APPETIZER

Slice on a sharp diagonal 1/2 inch
thick:
**large celery stalks to make
1 pint**
Sauté celery, covered, until just
tender in:
**1 tablespoon garlic olive oil,
heated**
Combine:
1 tablespoon vinegar
1 teaspoon anchovy paste
Pour over celery to coat well.
Transfer to small chafing dish or
other warmer and serve immediately sprinkled with:
**4 tablespoons finely chopped
parsley**
paprika
Serves 12 as hors d'oeuvre

Parsley

MUSHROOMS IN BUTTERMILK SAUCE

Melt until bubbly:
3 tablespoons butter
Sprinkle with:
3 tablespoons flour
Cook and stir 3 minutes. Gradually add:
3/4 pint buttermilk
4 tablespoons dried onion flakes
1/4 to 1/2 teaspoon dry mustard
1/4 teaspoon each salt, freshly grated nutmeg and freshly ground white pepper
Cook and stir until thickened. Add:
3/4 pound small fresh mushrooms, with tough part of stems removed
Cook, covered, over medium heat until mushrooms are tender. Add:
2 to 2-1/2 ounces finely chopped parsley
Thin with more buttermilk if needed and adjust seasonings. Serve over toast points or as an accompaniment to meat.
Serves 3 to 6

ROOT BORSHCH

Sauté until slightly browned in:
4 tablespoons butter and/or rendered beef fat
1 large carrot, chopped
1 large onion, chopped
3 leeks, white only, chopped
1/2 pound lean salt pork, diced
4 tablespoons chopped parsley
Add:
2-1/2 to 3 pounds beef brisket or meaty short ribs, cut up
4 pints water
10 peppercorns, crushed
1 teaspoon salt
2 bay leaves
Cover, bring to gentle boil and cook 2 to 2-1/2 hours until meat is tender. Strain, dice and reserve meat; chill stock and remove fat.
Sauté until soft in:
4 tablespoons butter and/or rendered beef fat
1 onion, chopped
1 carrot, chopped
2 garlic cloves, finely chopped
Add:
6 beetroots, coarsely grated (reserve 5 tablespoons)
2 roots Hamburg parsley, coarsely grated
1 turnip, coarsely grated
1/2 medium-size root celeriac, coarsely grated

Sprinkle with:
1 teaspoon sugar
Cook and stir until well coated and slightly brown. Add:
4 large ripe tomatoes, peeled, seeded and coarsely chopped
1/4 teaspoon freshly ground black pepper
2 pints of the reserved stock
Cover, bring to gentle boil and cook until vegetables are tender. Bring remaining stock to boil; add:
1 pound boiling potatoes, cut up if large
Boil until potatoes are almost done. Add:
1/2 pound finely shredded cabbage
Cook rapidly until cabbage is just tender. Return to rest of soup and add:
4 or 8 ounces reserved diced meat
1 teaspoon citric acid*
Wrap reserved grated beetroots in cheesecloth and squeeze out as much juice as possible to add color. Reheat and adjust with more citric acid, sugar and pepper. Just before serving sprinkle with:
finely chopped parsley
Pass bowls of whipped sour cream.
Serves 8 to 10 for main meal

*Citric acid is available from chemists. Or use lemon juice or wine vinegar to taste.

Primrose

(*Primula* species and cultivars)

PRIMROSE
Primula *species and cultivars*
Perennial ground cover or
suitable for bedding
8 to 10 inches in height
Fast grower
Propagate from seed or division
Light shade
Hardy
Leaves and flowers eaten
Flowers in spring
Yellow, pink and white flowers

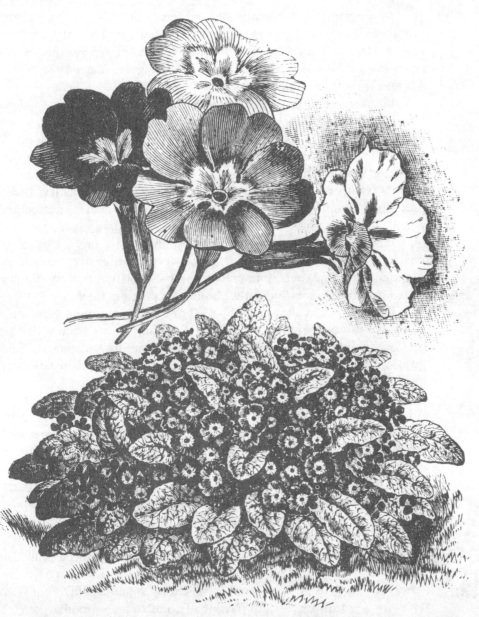

Primrose

In England in the early spring, the hedgerows are filled with primroses and every flower shop and garden has a variety of these simple, elegant flowers of easy culture. Primulas of various species also grace the gardens of Japan, China, Tibet, Mongolia, Yugoslavia, Labrador and the United States.

Popularly known as the primrose, cowslip or oxlip, these ubiquitous plants have their own mythological origin and, like so many edible herbs, were first popular as medicines. Flora, the goddess of flowers, and Priapus, the god of male procreative power, had a son, Parilisos, who expired of grief when his beloved died. Thereupon his parents transformed him into the rare primrose. Early medical books prescribed primroses as a cure for paralysis, women's chatter and burns; in the mouth to restore speech; with lard as a cosmetic ointment to "take away spots, wrinkles, and sunburnings." Engulfed in steam produced by pouring primrose-steeped water over hot stones, a patient could expect miraculous results. North American Indians prized the roots for eating, either boiling or pickling them.

Propagation in the spring by seed or division is simple. Sow seeds in a leafy mixture kept moist and cool. Young plants from a flat are best when allowed to develop in pots before transferring to final positions. Parent plants can be lifted, separated, and then replanted directly where you want them.

Primroses prefer high-humus, moist, deep soil in semi-shade. Adding moss peat or well-rotted compost will promote colorful spring flowering that will last about six weeks. If lower stems are then removed and plants are protected against snails and slugs, the leaves will remain attractive until winter comes. Keep free of weeds, though extensive cultivation is not needed.

Spray for aphids, if necessary, and protect with glass or plastic in early spring if extra flowers are desired. If left undivided more than three years, you may find many leaves but no flowers.

The primrose is an unusually versatile plant. It can be grown in the open, as a house plant or in a greenhouse and admired for its beauty alone. It is not commonly thought of as being edible, but both its leaves and flowers can add flavor and color to many foods.

BRAISED STUFFED MUSHROOMS

Soften in warm water to cover:
**24 medium uniform-size dried
     wild mushrooms***
Drain and dry. Cut out and
finely chop stems. Set aside.
Rub caps inside and out with:
1 tablespoon cornflour
Combine:
**chopped stems
1 pound lean pork, minced
6 to 8 tablespoons finely
     chopped ham
1 tablespoon each soy sauce,
     sherry and cornflour
1 tablespoon chopped primrose
     petals
1 tablespoon corn oil**
Fill caps with meat mixture,
pressing in firmly. Brown
meat side down in:
1 tablespoon corn oil
Turn caps meat side up and add:
**generous 1/4 pint chicken stock
1 tablespoon each soy sauce
     and sherry**
*Or use large, flat, cultivated fresh
 mushrooms.

Cover and cook over medium
heat 20 minutes. Thicken if
desired with binder of:
**2 tablespoons water
1 tablespoon cornflour**
Transfer to heated platter and
sprinkle with:
**4 tablespoons slivered spring
     onions and tops**
Makes 24 appetizers

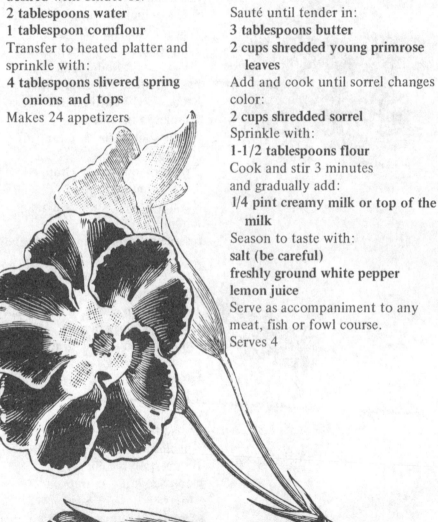

PRIMROSE LEAVES WITH SORREL

Sauté until tender in:
**3 tablespoons butter
2 cups shredded young primrose
     leaves**
Add and cook until sorrel changes
color:
2 cups shredded sorrel
Sprinkle with:
1-1/2 tablespoons flour
Cook and stir 3 minutes
and gradually add:
**1/4 pint creamy milk or top of the
     milk**
Season to taste with:
**salt (be careful)
freshly ground white pepper
lemon juice**
Serve as accompaniment to any
meat, fish or fowl course.
Serves 4

Primrose

PRIMROSE STUFFED SQUID

Remove fins, edible part of head and tentacles from:

1-1/2 pounds cleaned uniformly-sized small squid

Chop fins, head and tentacles finely. Drain bodies and dry with paper towels. Set both aside. Sauté slowly until tender in:

2 tablespoons olive oil

8 tablespoons finely chopped onion

2 tablespoons finely chopped chive bulbs (page 62)

Raise heat and sauté, stirring, 2 minutes:

reserved chopped fins, heads and tentacles

3 tablespoons chopped parsley

Season with:

1/4 teaspoon each salt and freshly ground white pepper

1/8 teaspoon freshly grated nutmeg

Sprinkle with:

2 tablespoons flour

Cook and stir 3 minutes and add:

4 tablespoons dry white wine

8 tablespoons milk

Cook and stir 5 minutes and add:

scant 1-1/2 ounces fresh fine bread crumbs

Continue cooking 10 minutes, stirring often and adding more bread crumbs until stuffing is very thick. Stir in:

5 tablespoons finely chopped primrose petals

Adjust seasonings and chill. Stuff squid bodies and secure ends with toothpicks. Sprinkle lightly with:

flour

Brown quickly on all sides in:

2 tablespoons each olive oil and butter

Squid will shrink up; do not overcook. Remove and set aside. To frying pan add:

4 tablespoons flour

Cook and stir 3 minutes and then gradually add:

1/2 pint each milk and rich parsley chicken stock (page 28)

Cook and stir until smooth and very thick. Return squid to sauce, cover and cook, turning squid once, 8 to 10 minutes. Do not overcook. Squid will add more moisture to sauce. If too thick, add:

milk or chicken stock

Remove squid and toss sauce with:

1/2 pound fresh narrow noodles, cooked al dente

Remove to serving platter and top with squid. Sprinkle with:

finely chopped parsley

Serves 3 to 4

PRIMROSE LEAF
GREEN NOODLES

Sift on to large board
9 ounces unbleached flour
1/2 teaspoon salt
Make hollow in center and add:
2 eggs
1 teaspoon corn oil
With fingers, using spatula to
bring flour from edges, gradually
blend eggs and oil into flour.
When almost blended knead in:
6 tablespoons finely chopped
cooked primrose leaves,
squeezed dry
When thoroughly blended and
smooth form into a ball, cover
with slightly dampened towel and
let rest 20 minutes. Divide into
4 equal portions and roll each as
thinly as possible, using flour if
needed. Place each sheet on
floured greaseproof paper. Let dry
only as long as it takes to roll
entire batch. Starting with first
sheet, roll up half the sheet
toward the center like a Swiss
roll; then roll the other half
toward the center until they
meet in the middle. With a very
sharp knife cut into desired
widths; with blunt edge of knife
lift at center fold and shake
strips free. Hang strips over the
back of a chair until all dough

is used. Cook within 10 minutes
in a large pot of boiling salted
water to which 1 or 2 teaspoons
corn oil have been added. Cook
only until tender. Drain and
dress with sauce or butter. If you
wish to prepare the dough ahead
of time, lay strips on floured
greaseproof paper, roll up and seal,
using more flour if needed to
prevent strips from sticking
together. Or place on floured
baking sheets, freeze and wrap.
Swiss chard may be substituted
for the primrose leaves.
Serves 6

SERVING HINTS

• Prepare a primrose salad using
both the tender leaves and flowers.
• The leaves can also be cooked
and served as a potherb, or mixed
with other herbs as a stuffing for
meat and poultry.
• Use the flowers in a conserve
or tart, or candy them for an
attractive garnish.
• Make primrose syrup or tea
with leaves or flowers.
• Prepare an interesting and
delicate-flavored boiled custard
with the flowers.

Pyracantha

(Pyracantha angustifolia and *Pyracantha coccinea)*

PYRACANTHA
Pyracantha angustifolia *and*
Pyracantha coccinea
Evergreen shrub or small tree
10 to 12 feet in height
Fast grower
Propagate from cuttings or seed
Sun
Hardy
Berries eaten
Flowers in late spring
Harvest in late summer
White flowers, red berries

A sturdy bush with fiery red berries and sharp, stout thorns, the pyracantha has been well named from the Greek *pyr* (fire) and *ácantha* (thorn). Many an unwary gardener has found fire in the thorns as well as in the brilliant color of the berries.

When introduced in England from Southern Europe in 1629, pyracantha quickly became a garden favorite because of its showy blossoms and berries. However, this variety was largely supplanted by prettier Chinese varieties, introduced in Europe in 1889 and widening in popularity around the turn of the century because of the efforts of plant hunter George Forrest.

Pyracantha can easily be grown from ripe seeds sown in autumn or cuttings taken in early spring. Well-drained soil in full sun is best. Given shade, the plants tend to grow more, but less stoutly. No special cultivation is needed, and fireblight is almost the only disease to be concerned about. The tips of the leaves turn brown, and affected branches should be cut back hard at once. Badly attacked bushes should be removed and replaced.

To train as an espalier or small tree, cut out all branches except those suitable for the shape desired. Side branches, if cut back to spurs one or two inches long, will produce flowers and berries to clothe the main stems each year.

There are many varieties of pyracantha, including a ground-cover type. Let your nurseryman help you decide which is best for your chosen location.

This hardy shrub, mantled with white blossoms in the spring and early summer, produces its edible orange to brick-red fruit in autumn. Many is the robin who has become drunk on the mature, fermented berries that stay on into the winter months in moderate climates. Pick the berries, being careful of the thorns, and wash well, removing the large stems; it is not necessary to remove all of the small stems when cooking down for jelly or sauce. The pyracantha fruit does not have the strong, distinctive flavor of other berries so that it is best to add an ingredient, grapefruit juice in the case of making jelly, to heighten the fruit's flavor. Pyracantha sauce complements such foods as baked sweet potatoes, cold lamb, hamburgers, hot dogs and poultry dishes.

PYRACANTHA JELLY

Combine and bring to boil:
**4 cups slightly underripe
   pyracantha berries**
5 cups water
Cover (tilt lid slightly) and cook
over medium heat 40 minutes.
Mash berries lightly and transfer
to jelly bag as directed on page
59. There should be approximately 2 cups juice. Add to the
juice:
1/4 cup grapefruit juice
2 tablespoons lemon juice
1 cup sugar
Continue following directions
for making jelly and start testing
after 10 minutes of cooking.

CHICKEN POACHED IN PYRACANTHA JELLY

Sauté in:
**2 tablespoons butter and/or
   rendered chicken fat**
**8 tablespoons finely chopped
   onion**
1 teaspoon finely chopped garlic
Season with:
salt
freshly ground white pepper
paprika
4 large chicken legs and thighs
Place in sauté pan with:
4 tablespoons rich chicken stock
Cover and simmer 10 minutes.
Add:
**8 tablespoons pyracantha jelly
   (see preceding)**
Cover and cook, stirring to dis-
tribute jelly and adding more
stock if needed, until chicken
is almost tender. Then add:
1 green pepper, cut in chunks
1 large onion, cut in eighths
Cover and continue cooking until
vegetables are tender but still
crisp. Serve over white or brown
rice, bulghur (cracked) wheat or
barley.
Serves 4

Quince

AND ORNAMENTAL QUINCE

(Cydonia oblonga and *Chaenomeles japonica* and cultivars)*

The quince was once dedicated to Venus as an emblem of love, happiness and fruitfulness. It decorated the bed chambers of Greek and Roman brides and grooms who ate the fruit after the marriage was performed. Even an ancient statue of Hercules had three quinces in his hand. Alleged by some to be Eden's forbidden golden fruit, it was probably native to ancient Crete, though recorded cultivation dates back in the Mediterranean region only to 1573.

Golden yellow when ripe in early autumn, the fruit of quince exudes a fine, rich odor distinctive from the pear, to which it's often compared. Mawes' *Dictionary of Gardening* says it "merits culture in every curious collection, some for fruit, some for ornament." (Though the flowering quince is not of the same genus, both types produce fruit and are treated the same.) The white or pink flowers appear in early spring.

Propagation can be by layering, by cuttings or by planting some of the abundantly produced suckers. In a sunny situation with well-drained soil, quince will thrive as well as in Crete without special care and with minimal treatment for pests and diseases. It may be grown as a low or tall shrub, an espalier or a tree up to 25 feet tall. If planted as a tree, a single stem must be selected and cut at the desired height for branches to form.

Pick quince when underripe and yellowish green in color and set out, not touching, to ripen. When they are a perfect, even yellow and very fragrant, they are ready to use and should be eaten or preserved immediately. Once ripe, the meat of the fruit will quickly become mealy. Those who have little experience with quince may find them difficult to work with at first. With practice, coring and seeding the fruit will become easier. Quince can be cooked down into a chutney, conserve or marmalade. They can also be served spiced or combined with apples in a tart or pie. When making quince jelly, do not peel the fruit or remove the pips; they are beneficial to setting of the jelly. Cream cheese is a good accompaniment to quince preserves.

QUINCE JELLY

In a large pan, combine:
**20 large cooking apples, cut in
    eighths**
12 large quinces, quartered
3 pints red currants
Cover with water and boil until
soft. Place in jelly bag as directed
on page 59, and continue to
follow directions, adding for
each cup of juice:
1 cup sugar
Work with only 3 or 4 cups of
juice at a time. Pour into hot,
sterilized half-pint jars, seal and
store in a cool, dry place.

QUINCE AND APPLE ROLL

Toss to coat thoroughly:
**1-1/2 cups finely chopped, peeled
    and cored quince**
**1 cup finely chopped, peeled
    and cored apples**
**1/2 cup currants or finely
    chopped raisins**
**1 cup (about 7 ounces) brown
    sugar**
1/2 teaspoon cinnamon
1/4 teaspoon allspice

Sift together:
9 ounces unbleached flour
2 tablespoons castor sugar
2 teaspoons baking powder
1 teaspoon salt
Cut in until crumbly:
2 ounces butter
With fork, stir in:
1/4 pint milk
Form a ball, flatten slightly on
floured board and roll into a
rectangle 1/8 inch thick and
approximately 12 by 13 inches.
Cover with fruit mixture within
3/4 inch of sides. Dot with:
**2 ounces butter, cut into
    small bits**
Starting with short end, roll
tightly like Swiss roll. Place seam
side down on buttered and lightly
floured Swiss roll tin. Bake in
350° oven for 40 minutes or until
golden. Transfer to serving plate
and serve warm with:
**vanilla ice cream or
    sweetened whipped cream**
Top with:
slightly sweetened mulberries
Serves 12 to 16

QUINCE CHUTNEY

In heavy saucepan combine:
**2 cups each diced peeled and
    cored quince and apples**
**1 cup each raisins and chopped
    onion**
2 cups brown sugar
**1 cup each cider vinegar and
    apple juice**
**1/2 to 1 tablespoon finely
    chopped ginger root**
**1/2 to 1 tablespoon crushed dried
    hot peppers**
1 tablespoon mustard seed
1 3-inch piece cinnamon, broken
3/4 teaspoon salt
Stirring constantly, bring to boil.
Lower heat and continue cooking
slowly 1 hour or until very thick.
Stir often to prevent sticking.
Pour into hot sterilized jars and
seal.
Makes approximately 3 cups

For conserve: add 1 cup chopped
walnuts.

Raspberry

(*Rubus idaeus* and cultivars)

The raspberry, a species of the large *Rosaceae* or rose family, has long been cultivated for its succulent fragile fruit. It deserves a place in the ornamental garden, especially when espaliered for its brambly form, and its modest flowers which promise a harvest to come. Native to much of Europe, hardy and rapid growing, raspberries were brought into cultivation at the close of the Middle Ages. Introduced to North America by the early 1800's, raspberries quickly spread largely due to their popularity with birds who readily transported the seeds. All the many varieties are best grown from suckers, thus assuring the special qualities of the parent plant.

Good open loam, well drained and high in humus, produces the best fruit. Plants, planted in full sun, should be dressed each year with well-rotted compost or manure. If this is not available, feed with any fertilizer recommended for roses. Moisture is important and plants should never be dry, especially when the fruit is swelling.

In winter cultivate well and prune simultaneously, removing at ground level the canes with branches that have already fruited and leaving straight first-year canes for branching and fruiting the second year. At this time, also train remaining canes on wire to espalier.

In certain areas raspberries are particularly attractive to caterpillars. If they start to devour the leaves, spray with an insecticide with short toxicity.

Buy your choice of the many varieties from a well-established nursery knowledgeable in local climate conditions.

Ready to eat when they easily pull from the canes, raspberries are high in vitamin C and delicately flavored. When ripe they have a bright, clean even color and a plump appearance; when overripe, the color dulls and the berry splits and leaks juice. Raspberries combine well with strawberries, peaches and apricots.

RASPBERRY
Rubus idaeus and cultivars
Deciduous perennial
Height depends on support; normally no more than 8 to 10 feet
Fast grower
Propagate from suckers
Sun
Hardy
Berries eaten
Flowers in spring
Harvest in summer
White and pink flowers, red berries

Raspberry

SERVING HINTS

• Serve with crushed pineapple and macaroons, ice cream and whipped cream.
• Combine with cream cheese, sugar and vanilla as a dessert crêpe filling; dot with butter, heat and serve with raspberry sauce.
• Marinate raspberries and cantaloupe balls in kirsch or Grand Marnier and chill.
• Use sour cream sweetened with brown sugar or cream cheese softened with brandy as a topping for fresh-picked berries.
• Prepare hollowed-out orange cups, pile with raspberries combined with a little sugar, grated orange or lemon rind, orange juice and chopped mint, and garnish with tiny mint sprigs.
• Flavor vinegar with raspberries.
• Make jams and jellies to serve with toast, or to use as filling for pies and glazes for tarts.

RASPBERRY MERINGUE PIE

Beat until stiff:
4 egg whites
1/4 teaspoon cream of tartar
1/2 teaspoon cider vinegar
Gradually beat in:
6 ounces castor sugar
Continue beating until stiff, smooth and glossy. Transfer to round baking dish about 9 inches in diameter and 2 to 3 inches deep. Spread to cover center of dish with meringue about 1 inch deep and build meringue along sides of dish about 1-1/2 to 2 inches thick. Bake in 225° oven 1-1/4 hours until just starting to turn golden. Cool and set aside.
In top of double boiler, beat:
4 egg yolks
4 ounces castor sugar
1 teaspoon grated lime peel
5 to 6 tablespoons lime juice
Cook, stirring constantly, over simmering water 20 minutes or until thickened. Mixture should stay away from sides of pan. Do not overcook. Cool and fold in:
4 ounces raspberries, slightly crushed
8 fluid ounces double cream, whipped
Pour over meringue, cover and chill 20 to 24 hours. Just before serving spread over filling:
4 fluid ounces double cream, whipped with
2 tablespoons castor sugar
Top with:
whole raspberries
grated lime peel
Serves 6 to 8

COLESLAW WITH RASPBERRIES

Combine:
1/4 pint sour cream
2 tablespoons top of the milk
1 tablespoon each mayonnaise and cider vinegar
2 teaspoons sugar
1-1/4 pounds finely shredded cabbage
salt and white pepper to taste
Chill and just before serving toss in:
6 ounces raspberries
Serves 6

FIGS WITH RASPBERRY SAUCE

Peel and chill:
16 to 24 fresh figs
Crush and press through medium sieve:
12 ounces raspberries
4 tablespoons castor sugar
Whip until just starting to thicken:
1/2 pint double cream
4 tablespoons icing sugar
Add the sieved raspberries and:
1 tablespoon kirsch or other liqueur
Place figs in 8 serving dishes and pour sauce over. Garnish with:
6 ounces whole raspberries
Serves 8

Rhubarb

(Rheum rhaponticum)

Rhubarb leaves, giants in the plant world, and rhubarb's yellow-green flowers reaching up to six feet, can add a "tropical" touch to many a northern garden. The rhubarb's rootlike subterranean stems, or rhizomes, have been noted for their medicinal qualities—cathartic and astringent—as far back as 2700 B.C. in China. It wasn't until around A.D. 1800 that the edible stalks of the *Rheum rhaponticum* species, a native of the eastern Mediterranean, became popular in England and New England for making sauce, tarts and pies.

Fresh rhubarb seeds can be sown in early autumn in well-drained open soil (under trees if desired) in drills three feet apart and one inch deep, though it will take at least two years to produce edible stalks. To be preferred is propagation by planting crowns in early spring surrounded by well-rotted manure or rich compost. Even then it's best not to pull stalks until plants are completely established, else the crown will be damaged. Keep soil well fed and watered, and protect against snails and slugs. Remove stems cleanly to avoid crown rot.

Adult plants need composting over the winter as well as lifting, dividing, and replanting every four years to maintain young growth. If the kitchen takes first priority, remove flowers to prevent bitterness in the stalks. Alternatively, the decorative flower heads can be left and enjoyed without hurting the plant, and then new seeds can be harvested for additional autumn planting.

Although rhubarb is actually a vegetable, it is used mainly in the manner of a fruit. Due to its versatility, it combines well with strawberries, bananas, pineapple, dates, oranges and quince.

SERVING HINTS

• Cook rhubarb with thin slices of unpeeled orange and sweeten with honey.
• Peel stalks lightly and cut them up to cook in flans, pies and crumbles.
• Stew rhubarb for sauces, jellies, jams and marmalades; sprinkle with one-half as much sugar as rhubarb, let stand 8 hours or more and cook in a saucepan or bake in a slow oven without additional water.
• Use rhubarb sauce for making ice cream or as an ice cream topping, in brown Betty or shortcake, or in cooking chicken or turkey.

RHUBARB FLOWERS

Rhubarb leaves are poisonous, but the flowers are good deep fried. Soak the blossoms 30 minutes in salted water, drain, dip in batter and deep fry. Sprinkle with icing sugar and serve.

RHUBARB BREAD/MUFFINS*

In blender purée:
10 ounces diced rhubarb
2 eggs
1/4 pint salad oil
Sift together:
5 ounces unbleached flour
5 ounces castor sugar
1 teaspoon each soda, baking
   powder and cinnamon
1/2 teaspoon salt
1/4 teaspoon allspice
Stir into rhubarb and pour into a well-buttered and lightly floured loaf tin or 16 patty pans. Bake in 350° oven 1 hour (35 to 40 minutes for muffins) or until golden, toothpick inserted in center comes out clean and bread pulls away from sides of tin. Turn out on to rack to cool. Serve warm or at room temperature with butter or softened cream cheese.
Makes 1 loaf, 16 muffins
*This makes a good pudding served with a fruit or custard sauce.

Rhubarb

RHUBARB POPOVERS

In blender combine and mix well:
2 eggs
1/4 teaspoon salt
1 cup milk
1 cup flour
Cover and refrigerate at least 40 minutes. Butter 6 popover tins and chill thoroughly. Place tins on baking sheet and fill with
1 tablespoon batter. Combine:
6 tablespoons finely diced rhubarb
1 tablespoon icing sugar
Divide rhubarb between tins and fill each with remaining batter. Place in cold oven and turn heat to 425°. Bake 45 minutes or until golden. *Do not open oven door first 30 minutes.* Remove from tins and serve immediately with butter.
Makes 6 popovers

CHICKEN GORGONZOLA HORS D'OEUVRE

Combine:
4 tablespoons sake or dry sherry
2 tablespoons soy sauce
2 slices ginger root, slivered
1 garlic clove, chopped
In above mixture marinate
3 hours, turning often:
1 pair large chicken breasts

Transfer to heavy saucepan and cook 10 minutes per side with a little marinade and:
2 tablespoons butter
Cool, skin, bone and slice thinly lengthwise.
Combine:
2 ounces Gorgonzola cheese, crumbled
1 ounce cream cheese, softened
Spread on chicken slices, sandwich together and cut into squares. Spear each sandwich with a wooden toothpick or skewer. Finish with:
square of rhubarb cooked slightly with tiny bit of sugar, or
seeded red dessert grape half
Place on baking sheet and drizzle with:
equal parts soy sauce and honey, heated
Bake in 350° oven 5 minutes or until heated through. Serve immediately.
Makes approximately 30

RHUBARB SALAD MOULD

In heavy saucepan combine:
1 pound finely chopped rhubarb
6 fluid ounces each water and orange juice
3 ounces sugar
Cover tightly and simmer, stirring occasionally, until rhubarb is tender. Then add:
1/4 teaspoon each allspice and red food coloring
Soften in:
3 tablespoons cold water
1 envelope gelatine
Dissolve in hot rhubarb and refrigerate until almost set, stirring often. Fold in:
4 ounces each sliced bananas and strawberries
1/4 pint double cream, whipped until just starting to thicken
Pour into ring mould that has been rinsed in cold water. Cover and refrigerate 6 hours until set. Unmould on chilled serving platter and sprinkle with:
grated orange peel
Surround with lettuce cups and fill center with creamy mayonnaise if desired.
Serves 6 to 8

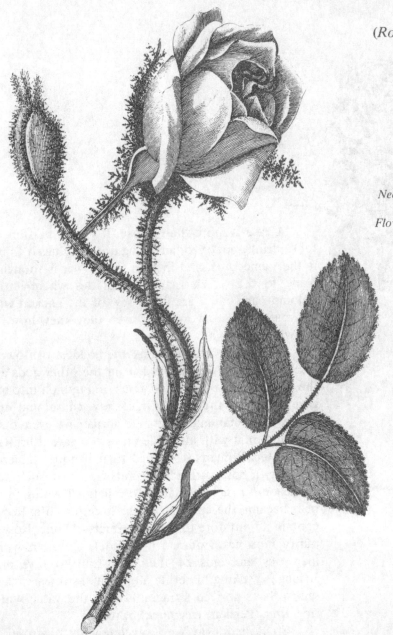

Rose

(*Rosa* species and cultivars)

ROSE
Rosa species and cultivars
Sometimes evergreen,
perennial shrub
Height depends on variety
Fast grower
Propagate from cuttings or
buy budded plants
Sun
Needs protection in colder areas
Flowers eaten
Flowers in late spring or summer
Various colors

Rose

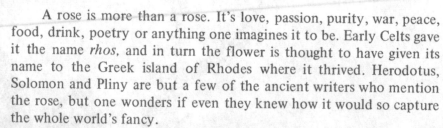

A rose is more than a rose. It's love, passion, purity, war, peace, food, drink, poetry or anything one imagines it to be. Early Celts gave it the name *rhos*, and in turn the flower is thought to have given its name to the Greek island of Rhodes where it thrived. Herodotus, Solomon and Pliny are but a few of the ancient writers who mention the rose, but one wonders if even they knew how it would so capture the whole world's fancy.

Mythology bids us thank the goddess of flowers, Chloris, for the rose. It was she who evoked from the other gods a transformation of the outstanding beauty and grace of a nymph into a flower. Aphrodite gave it beauty; the Three Graces joy, charm and brilliance. Dionysius bestowed nectar and fragrance surpassing even that of wine. Apollo smiled upon it with his golden rays and gave it brilliance.

Later, Romans festooned their banquet tables and adorned their heads with rose garlands. Secrets heard on such occasions were considered *sub rosa*—inviolate. Rose petals floating in wine or strewn on beds became the epitome of the luxurious life. Roses were thought to contain an antidote to the evil effects of wine. Rose water was used to purify mosques profaned by infidels. Cavaliers wore roses at tournaments as emblems of their devotion to love and beauty. Caliph Jehangir, walking his bride along petal-strewn canals and fountains, is said to have noticed a fragrant oil on the water, which he bottled—the first *attar* (Persian: fragrance) of roses.

So carried away was everyone with "the rose" that no one seems to have scientifically classified the many early varieties found in

Rose

almost every Northern Hemisphere country. Hybridizers, of course, have long been busy developing new colors and forms, yet it is still difficult to find a hybrid more graceful than some of the wild species woven into the tapestry of fable, legend and history. An example is the red and white rose emblem of England. Called the Tudor rose, it was adopted after the House of York (white rose) and the House of Lancaster (red rose) ceased their feuding. This Tudor rose was also found on British coinage.

No garden should be without a rose or two, or more. No matter which variety you choose, the history of this noble flower belongs in part to all. Rose culture has become a complicated field all its own, the subject of hundreds of books and articles, but the basic rules are not difficult.

Most modern roses are propagated by budding onto hardy stocks raised from seed. *Rosa multiflora* and *R. canina* are two of the stocks used. If only the more robust rose varieties are used, successful plants can be started from moderately thick, hard-wood cuttings, eight to 10 inches long. Place cuttings in sandy soil so that the stems are two-thirds covered. The lower cut should be just below a node (where a leaf emerges from the stem), the higher cut just above another node. Alternatively, a cutting taken in August of new growth with a "heel" of old wood can be placed in a frame for rooting in a few weeks, then potted until large enough to plant. Many shrubby types can be lifted in autumn, divided and portions with roots replanted. Less robust varieties do not do well on their own roots, so rather than tackle the difficult task of propagation by budding and grafting on stronger plants, one is advised to buy such varieties started in a nursery.

Roses like full sun in cooler climates, semi-shade in hot areas, and adequate moisture but not "wet feet" during the growing season. Well-worked clay is ideal, with plenty of humus or rotted manure added if the soil is not naturally rich in organic matter. Specially blended rose fertilizers are necessary for feeding established plants. During the growing season, hoe out weeds and add a top dressing of organic compost to retain moisture in the summer. Grass clippings spread around the base should not be too thick so they decompose easily. Such a mulch helps control black spot.

Rose

Choose your favorite colors—they're almost unlimited—as climbers, standards or bush roses to fit the site. Then keep under control by appropriate training. Pruning should be done in early spring before new growth starts, using the following tactics.

- Remove dead wood and weak shoots and cut back to an outside bud.
- Cut out older canes of bush roses to 12 to 20 inches. Leave half of them longer than the others to be removed the next year.
- Try to keep the center open to inhibit mildew and rust.
- Cut back standard roses to three or four buds from main branches.
- Each year prune out older shoots severely and selectively to encourage new growth.

Should mildew or rust persist, spray with fungicide. Frequently the spores of rust and black spot are soil borne and are spread to plants by splashes of water during rain or watering. Mulching minimizes the splashes.

If aphids are a problem, try garlic spray (page 19). If this doesn't work, proceed to chemicals, but be wary of those insecticides harmful to roses and avoid those not specifically recommended as safe for use on food crops.

Unless your mind is already made up or you want to fall back on the old-time favorite Peace, you'd best consult your nurseryman on which roses best meet your desires and growing conditions. Otherwise the multiplicity of available varieties may prove to be overwhelming.

In culinary history, no other flower can match the attention given the rose. Numerous books and articles have been written on the use of both rose petals and rose hips in cookery. When selecting roses for cooking, choose the darkest, most fragrant ones as they have the most flavor. Gather the flowers before the sun is on them. Pull off the petals and remove the green or white heel that is attached to the flower base. Wash petals, dry between paper towels and use immediately. When cooking, use only enamel, glass or stainless steel pots and a wooden spoon for stirring.

SERVING HINTS

- Place rose petals in the bottom of a cake tin before pouring in cake batter.
- Add chopped petals to an omelette seasoned with celery salt and fresh marjoram.
- Dip petals in batter to which brandy or rose water has been added and deep fry.
- Steep petals in brandy for 3 to 4 weeks and use the brandy in custards, puddings, dessert sauces and for flaming dishes.
- Crystallize petals and place on top of cherries in a cherry pie, or garnish cakes, fruit salads or desserts.
- Chopped petals enhance the flavor of custards, puddings, pancake and muffin batters.
- Use rose petal sugar, water or syrup in baklava, custards, ice cream, icings, candy creams or marzipan with kirsch added, or when poaching fish.
- Mix rose water or syrup with honey, butter, anise and saffron as a basting sauce for roast chicken or other fowl.
- Make rose butter and substitute it for unflavored butter in cakes or gingerbread, or in sandwiches.

SIAMESE ROSE PETAL SALAD

Cut into long, thin strands:
petals from 2 dark fragrant roses
Combine with:
**6 ounces each shredded cooked
    chicken and pork**
1-1/2 tablespoons hoisin sauce*
**6 to 8 tablespoons shredded
    spring onions and tops**
1/2 teaspoon sesame oil (extract)*
2 tablespoons lemon juice
**2 tablespoons each finely
    chopped peanuts and toasted
    sesame seeds**
Toss to mix well and set aside.
Fry in hot corn oil, a few handfuls
at a time, until just golden:
**1/4 pound py mei fun (fine rice
    sticks)*, broken up**
Immediately drain rice sticks on
paper towels. (They will expand
about 10 times their size.) Toss
two-thirds of the py mei fun into
chicken pork mixture and arrange
on:
bed of shredded lettuce
Top with remaining py mei fun
and:
**1 tablespoon each finely chopped
    peanuts and toasted sesame
    seeds**

Deep fry until puffed:
shrimp chips*
Arrange around salad and serve
at room temperature as a luncheon dish with clear broth with
bean curd and peas and a dessert
of plain fruit or ice cream with
mangoes.
Serves 8 to 10

*Available in some Chinese
provision stores.

ROSE PETAL JAM

To make rose petal jam, combine
equal parts petals, sugar and
water. The petals can be either
left in or strained out after
cooking, and strawberry juice
may be added to enhance the
flavor. Whenever making jams or
jellies, it is a good idea to add
a little lemon juice and a touch
of cream of tartar at jelling time
to prevent bitterness.

Rose

ROSE PETAL CRÊPES

To Make Crêpes:
In blender blend until smooth:
2 eggs
1/4 pint milk
6 tablespoons unbleached flour
1/8 teaspoon salt
1/2 tablespoons castor sugar
1/2 tablespoon corn oil
Cover and refrigerate at least
2 hours.

To Make Filling:
In top of double boiler combine:
1/2 pint plus 3 tablespoons milk
2 eggs beaten
4 tablespoons rose sugar (page 28)
dash salt
4 tablespoons very finely chopped
   fragrant rose petals
Cook over simmering water,
stirring constantly, until custard
coats spoon. Then add:
1 teaspoon rose water
Cool and combine 6 tablespoons
custard with:
1 pound cottage cheese, creamed
6 tablespoons raisins
2 tablespoons rose honey
   (page 27)
1/2 teaspoon grated lemon or
   lime peel
1/8 teaspoon each cinnamon and
   freshly grated nutmeg
Refrigerate until ready to fill
crêpes.

Heat a 7-inch crêpe pan, butter
lightly and when butter bubbles
pour in about 3 tablespoons
crêpe batter. Quickly tip the pan
from side to side to coat entire
bottom. Cook until golden over
medium heat; turn and cook
other side 1 minute. While cooking crêpes, stir batter often,
adding more milk if too thick.
As each crêpe is cooked, stack
on a towel or rack. Place about
3 tablespoons cottage cheese
filling on one edge of crêpe and
roll. Place in well-buttered
shallow baking dish. At this point
crêpes may be refrigerated.
When ready to serve, dot crêpes
with:
3 tablespoons butter
Heat in 350° oven 10 minutes or
until heated through. Heat
remaining custard in double
boiler and pour over crêpes.
Sprinkle with:
1 tablespoon grated orange peel
Makes 10 crêpes

Rose

COUSCOUS STUFFING FOR POULTRY

Bring to boil:
2 cups water
1/2 teaspoon salt
2 tablespoons butter
Gradually sprinkle in:
1 cup couscous
Stirring occasionally, cook 4 minutes or until almost all water is absorbed. Remove from heat, cover tightly and let stand 10 minutes. Fluff with fork and toss in:
6 tablespoons each chopped raisins and blanched almonds
1/4 teaspoon each turmeric and cinnamon
1/8 teaspoon each powdered ginger, cumin and powdered cloves
3 to 4 tablespoons rose honey (page 27)
1 tablespoon chopped leaves from rose honey
salt and white pepper to taste
This recipe makes enough stuffing for a 3-pound chicken.

ROSE HIPS

Rose hips, the berry or fruit left after the flower has withered, are very high in vitamin C, and also contain vitamins A, B, K and F. Rose hips must always be precooked before using them in recipes. Depending on the rose species, rose hips take from 1 to 3 hours of simmering in water to cook to a soft stage. Try making rose hip jelly or jam, adding if necessary a bit of cornflour or potato flour to eliminate the astringent taste of the fruit. For a truly healthful beverage, make a pot of rose hip tea.

ROSE HIP SOUP

Omit lemon juice in recipe for Rose Hip Sauce which follows. Thin with water and flavor with:
2 tablespoons Madeira or to taste
Float on top of each serving:
lemon slices
Sprinkle with:
toasted slivered almonds
Serves 2 to 3

ROSE HIP SAUCE

Bring to boil:
2 cups (about 3/4 pint) water
1 cup rose hips
Cover and cook gently 1 to 2 hours or until tender, adding more water if it boils away. Sieve, forcing as much pulp through as possible. If needed add more water to make 3/4 cup pulp. Return to saucepan and reheat..
Dissolve in:
1 tablespoon water
1/2 tablespoon cornflour
Add to rose hips and cook and stir until thickened, adding:
1 teaspoon lemon juice
3 to 4 tablespoons sugar
Adjust to taste and pour over:
hot cooked asparagus or broccoli
Sprinkle with:
3 to 4 tablespoons toasted slivered almonds
Also good as a hot dip for assorted raw vegetables.
Makes a generous 1/4 pint

Rosemary

(Rosmarinus officinalis)

ROSEMARY
Rosmarinus officinalis
Evergreen, perennial shrub
3 to 5 feet in height
Fast grower
Propagate from cuttings
Sun
Hardy
Foliage and flowers eaten
Flowers in spring
Blue flowers

Rosemary

Rosemary, a native of Europe and Asia Minor, centuries ago enjoyed a place of honor in folklore. It was called the herb of memory, for a brew of its leaves was purported to rekindle long lost thoughts. In Shakespeare's *Hamlet*, Ophelia says "there's rosemary, that's for remembrance." The Queen of Hungary once used "Hungary water" made with rosemary to keep her hair in curl. French confectioners have used rosemary honey in their candy and a rosemary liqueur is prized by connoisseurs. It has additionally earned a reputation as an ornamental, for its long-lived trunks become more decorative with age. It is a close relative and a fine companion to lavender in the garden.

To propagate, take six-inch cuttings in the spring, place them in a cold frame in well-drained soil and water well; they will root readily if protected from wind with a plastic cover until well rooted. Seeds germinate easily and also require early protection. A sunny location with light, well-drained soil is best for planting. Without special cultivation (but preventing build-up of debris under the plant), the rosemary can withstand all but the severest winters.

Pruning to keep the plant within bounds and to renew growth on older branches will add to its beauty. Rosemary, varieties of which cascade over low walls, makes a most attractive plant in and out of flower with its dark green leaves during the winter.

Aromatic and pungent, with a hint of pine, rosemary has been described as a "cross between sage and lavender with a touch of ginger and camphor." Some may consider its potentially overpowering flavor an acquired taste. Though it is generally best when used alone, it will blend successfully with some herbs such as thyme, marjoram and lavender for rubbing on a beef roast. Rosemary will add flavor to any number of foods, but because of its strong flavor should always be added sparingly, especially if dried. When adding dried rosemary to uncooked foods, soak it first in hot water.

SERVING HINTS

• Use rosemary to flavor cold drinks, soups, pickles, cooked meats, omelettes, egg casserole, fish and poultry, sauces, dressing, and even preserves and jams.

• Sauté chopped rosemary in butter, sprinkle with flour and add stock. Season with lemon juice and anchovy paste and serve on fish.

• Add chopped rosemary to fresh fruit compotes, to pastry for meat pies or to cake batter when making a traditional wedding cake.

• Cook orange sections in syrup, flavor with rosemary and vanilla essence to taste, chill and serve with whipped cream.

• Rub veal, pork or lamb roast with rosemary.

• Combine rosemary with butter to dress broad beans.

• Use whole sprigs with flowers for garnishing, or put them in the oven when baking bread.

• Add sprigs to the cooking water when boiling potatoes, or cooking Swiss chard or beans.

153

Rosemary

ROSEMARY BLOSSOMS

The pretty rosemary blossom is also edible. Flavor apple jelly with just a few flowers added to the jar before pouring in the hot jelly. Or infuse honey, white wine or vinegar with the blossoms to add a distinctive, pleasant taste.

PORK PATTIES

Sauté to stiffen in:
1 tablespoon butter
3 ounces pork liver
Finely chop and set aside.
Cover and cook until limp in:
2 tablespoons water
4 ounces finely chopped Swiss chard
Add and cook 2 minutes:
3 tablespoons white of leek or
1 teaspoon finely chopped garlic spring onion

Combine with reserved pork liver:
1 pound lean pork, minced
3 tablespoons finely chopped parsley
2 tablespoons finely chopped celery and leaves
3 tablespoons cornflour
2 tablespoons dry vermouth
1 teaspoon salt
1/2 teaspoon freshly ground black pepper
1/2 teaspoon very finely chopped rosemary or to taste
Sauté a small amount and adjust seasonings. Chill and form into 12 patties. Wrap each patty in:
caul fat*
Bake in 400° oven 25 minutes. Drain well on paper towels and serve hot or at room temperature.
Serves 6

*Caul fat is a fatty, net-like membrane from the pig. Paper-thin strips of bacon may be substituted, but the flavor will not be quite the same.

CROQUETTES

Sauté until soft but not browned in:
4 tablespoons olive oil
4 tablespoons finely chopped onion
1/4 teaspoon finely chopped garlic
1/4 teaspoon very finely chopped rosemary and flowers
Sprinkle with:
6 tablespoons flour
Cook and stir 3 minutes and gradually add:
3/4 pint evaporated milk
Cook and stir until thick. Add:
4 tablespoons flaked cooked fish
Cook, stirring often, 15 minutes. Adjust seasonings with:
salt
freshly ground white pepper
Cool and refrigerate. Form into small ovals and dip in:
beaten egg
Coat lightly with:
very fine bread crumbs
Chill 1 hour. Deep fry until golden in:
corn oil
Drain on paper towels and serve immediately.
Makes approximately 2 dozen

BARBECUED SALMON

Turning often, marinate 30 minutes in:
1/4 pound butter, melted
4 tablespoons each lemon juice, chopped onion and coarsely chopped parsley
1/2 to 1 teaspoon very finely chopped rosemary
1 5-pound whole salmon, cleaned with skin left on
Remove salmon from marinade and sprinkle inside and out with:
salt and freshly ground black pepper
Place on double sheet of heavy foil, pour marinade inside and over, and place on top of salmon:
4 slices lemon
4 parsley sprigs
Bring edges of foil up and around and cover loosely with another sheet of foil. Grill over medium coals, basting frequently, 50 minutes, or until fish flakes easily. Do not overcook. Discard lemon slices and parsley sprigs and transfer to platter. Garnish with:
hard-boiled egg slices
finely chopped chives
paprika
lemon wedges
Serve with:
browned butter
Serves 6

CREAMED ONIONS

In heavy saucepan cover and cook until tender:
24 small white onions, peeled
4 tablespoons lavender beef stock (page 28)
1 tablespoon butter
1 rosemary sprig
Discard rosemary sprig.
Melt until bubbly:
2 tablespoons butter
Sprinkle with:
2 tablespoons flour
Cook and stir 3 minutes and gradually add:
8 tablespoons asparagus or bean water
1/4 pint creamy milk or top of the milk
Cook and stir until smooth and thickened.
Add to sauce onions and any remaining juices. Serve with barbecued steak or in baked pastry shells as a garnish for any meat course.
Serves 4 as vegetable course, 6 as garnish

Sage

(Salvia officinalis)

Plants of the genus *Salvia* are found all over the world. But the sage commonly used in cooking is native to the Mediterranean. There the Roman physicians named it "the official saver" *(officinalis salvere),* because it was so highly prized as a medicine for the brain, nerves, stomach and female organs.

Sage has gradually lost its medical prestige, though its attractiveness, fragrance and spicy, slightly bitter taste have increased in favor as it proliferated throughout the world. The Old English saying, "He that would live for aye Must eat Sage in May," perhaps initiated a taste for sage tea as a healthful drink, and now some Orientals savor it as a beverage as much as more common teas. In Dalmatia its delicious honey commands the highest prices, and today few people, as they enjoy a sage stuffing with poultry or "heavy" meats such as pork, think of it as a means of preventing dyspepsia or as a remedy for vitamin A and C deficiencies during the winter months.

Over 500 *Salvia* species are known, including red sage, an annual, as well as white and variegated. Biennials and perennials are also included in the ranks of this genus. *S. officinalis* is an attractive grey color, and there are variegated and tricolor forms.

Sage is easily propagated in early summer by placing four-inch cuttings of young tips in sunny, sandy, alkaline soil. Sage is not too thirsty and likes plenty of room to itself. Pinch back frequently to form a compact plant. Like many herbs, it is free of most pests and diseases.

Like rosemary, sage, either dried or fresh, must be used with caution. The strong aromatic smell and the somewhat bitter, astringent taste are easily released and can overwhelm the foods in which this herb is used. Gather leaves from the young shoots near the top of the plant just before the flowers open, and use fresh or dry, or freeze them for later use. When drying, do not expose the leaves to the air for too long a period or they will lose their aroma. The flavor and aroma are retained best if the leaves are frozen rather than dried.

SERVING HINTS

- Chop leaves and add to butter or cream cheese for sandwiches, or to cottage cheese or soft Cheddar cheese for an appetizer spread.
- Combine with chives and chopped bacon for an omelette filling and garnish with a tiny sage sprig.
- Add to cooked vegetables, especially tomatoes, or to the pan when cooking meats, fish, chicken or calves' liver.
- Sage complements runner beans, stuffings for wild or domestic fowl and is a popular flavoring for sausage.

Sage

BUSECCA

In large heavy saucepan place:
1 onion, chopped
1 celery stalk and leaves, chopped
3 sage leaves
3 sprigs lemon thyme
2 large slices lemon peel
1-1/2 pounds dressed honeycomb
   tripe, cut into several pieces
Sprinkle with:
1/2 teaspoon salt
1/4 teaspoon freshly ground
   black pepper
Add, just to cover:
boiling water
Bring to gentle boil, cover and
simmer 30 minutes or until tripe
is tender. Remove tripe, cut into
bite-size pieces and reserve.

Sauté in:
2 tablespoons melted butter
1 small onion, thinly sliced
1 small carrot, thinly sliced
1 celery stalk, thinly sliced on
   diagonal
2 sage leaves, finely chopped
1/2 teaspoon sugar
Stir until golden. Then add:
1 large (28-ounce) can Italian
   peeled tomatoes, chopped
1/2 pint concentrated beef stock
Cover and cook 20 minutes. Add:
reserved tripe
1/2 pound cooked haricot beans
4 tablespoons finely chopped
   parsley
Cook, uncovered, 15 minutes.
Adjust seasonings and sprinkle
generously with:
grated Parmesan cheese
Serves 6 to 8

VENISON SAGE SAUSAGE

Using coarse blade of mincer,
mince:
1 pound venison
1/2 pound fatty bacon
1-1/2 to 2 teaspoons chopped sage
   leaves
Season with:
1/2 teaspoon salt
1/4 teaspoon black pepper
1/4 teaspoon dry mustard
   (optional)
1 tablespoon chopped chives
Add and blend well:
1 tablespoon water
Cover and chill overnight to blend
flavors. Put through mincer once
again. Then sauté a small
amount; adjust seasonings to
taste. Form patties and brown on
both sides to serve with apple-
sauce, eggs etc. Can also be used to
stuff cabbage rolls (page 110).
Makes 6 to 8 patties

OLIVETTES

Thaw in refrigerator overnight:
**About 12 ounces frozen puff
pastry**
Combine thoroughly:
2 pounds lean pork, minced
**2-1/2 ounces beef kidney fat
or suet, minced**
**6 to 8 tablespoons chopped
parsley**
2 eggs, beaten
3 tablespoons fine bread crumbs
4 tablespoons dry white wine
1-1/2 teaspoons chopped sage
1-1/2 teaspoons salt
**3/4 teaspoon freshly ground
black pepper**
Sauté a small amount and adjust
seasonings. Divide into 10 equal
portions.
Roll puff pastry 1/8 to 1/4 inch
thick. Cut into 10 6-inch rounds.
Place filling in center and encase with pastry, forming into
an olive shape. Place seam side
down on baking sheet and refrigerate 30 minutes. Bake in 400°
oven 10 minutes. Lower heat to
350° and bake 30 to 40 minutes
until golden. If pastry browns
too quickly in that time, cover
loosely with buttered paper.
Serve immediately or cool
and wrap loosely. Serve at room
temperature for picnic fare.
Makes 10

PORK CHOPS AND VEGETABLES WITH SAGE SAUCE

Trim:
6 thick pork chops
Sprinkle with:
1/2 teaspoon salt
**1/4 teaspoon freshly ground
black pepper**
paprika
Brown on all sides in:
**1 to 2 tablespoons garlic
olive oil**
Add:
**1/4 pint rich pork stock
(or substitute beef)**
Cover and simmer 15 to 20 minutes, adding more stock if needed.
Then add:
**12 to 18 small unpeeled red
potatoes**
Bring back to gentle boil, cover
and cook 10 minutes, depending
upon size of potatoes. Then add:
3/4 pound courgettes, sliced
Raise heat slightly and cook until
courgettes are just tender, adding
stock as needed. Adjust for salt
and pepper, arrange on heated
platter and pour following sauce
over chops and vegetables.
Sprinkle generously with:
finely chopped parsley
Serves 6

SAGE SAUCE

Sauté, covered, 10 minutes in:
2 tablespoons butter
**1 large Spanish onion
finely chopped**
**1 to 2 tablespoons finely
chopped sage**
Add:
5 tablespoons fine bread crumbs
Cook and stir 5 minutes. Then
add:
**1/4 pint rich pork stock (or sub-
stitute beef)**
Cover and cook gently 15 to 20
minutes, adding more stock as
needed. Season to taste with:
salt
freshly ground black pepper

Sorrel

(Rumex acetosa)

SORREL
Rumex acetosa
Herbaceous perennial ground cover
To 2 feet in height
Fast spreader
Propagate from seed or division
Light sun or shade
Hardy
Leaves eaten

The native English sorrel *(Rumex acetosa)* is not as known in cooking as the more bitter-tasting French species *(Rumex scutatus),* but *R. acetosa* deserves equal recognition in the kitchen and its use as a ground cover earns it a place in the ornamental garden. It is prized by both the Dutch and the French for its nutritive value, and in Holland acts as a substitute for spinach and as a pleasant addition to turnip greens.

Cultivation of sorrel for food markets dates back at least to 1596, though present-day varieties are considerably larger with more succulent leaves. As a ground cover, sorrel can be most effective if only the young, tender leaves are picked for the kitchen, leaving many others to provide a continuing soft, green covering. Easy to grow, it will extend beyond its bounds unless controlled.

Sow seeds in drill rows 15 inches apart or in the area to be covered in early spring. When the seedlings are three inches high, thin to 12 inches between plants. If watered well, the plants will thrive in good garden soil either in sun or partial shade. In the shade, the leaves tend to be more fleshy, but dense shade should be avoided.

Keep the ground well hoed, and protect against snails and slugs. Cutting for the kitchen can begin about two months after sowing. If left uncut, sorrel sends up two-foot shoots with pale green blossoms.

Known as sour grass or dock in the wild, sorrel has long been a favored herb of Europeans for imparting its lemony flavor to soups, sauces, salads and vegetable dishes. To prepare, remove stem and if leaves are large, cut out vein. Wash, dry, wrap in paper towels and refrigerate in a plastic bag until ready to use.

SERVING HINTS

- Leave sorrel leaves whole and add to spinach or turnip greens while they are cooking.
- Add fresh tender sorrel leaves to a tossed salad.
- Boil the leaves, add butter, a little sugar to bring out the flavor, salt and pepper and serve with roast goose or pork.
- Cook leaves with a little sugar, salt and pepper and purée; add a touch of vinegar and serve with cold meats.
- Chop fresh sorrel, steep in vinegar, drain and add to melted butter to serve with fish, scrambled eggs or hot potato salad.
- Combine chopped leaves with onion in an omelette and garnish with more chopped leaves.
- Use sorrel as a base for clear or cream soups and just before serving, sprinkle with a little freshly grated nutmeg.
- Add chopped leaves to seasoned cream sauce and bind with egg yolks or pan juices from roast being served.
- Stuff mushrooms with sorrel cream sauce, top with buttered bread crumbs and heat.

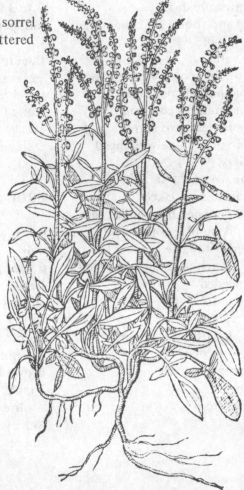

Sorrel

SORREL-CELERIAC SALAD

Boil 2 minutes or until barely
tender in:
salted water to cover
1 teaspoon lemon juice
1 large celeriac, peeled and
    uniformly diced
Drain and cook all moisture
away. Cool.
Toss with:
4 to 6 tablespoons mayonnaise
1 tablespoon lemon juice
about 6 ounces chopped
    tender leaves of sorrel
6 tablespoons finely chopped
    celery
1 7-ounce can tuna fish,
    drained and flaked
1 to 2 chopped hard-boiled eggs
salt and freshly ground white
    pepper to taste
mild French dressing to moisten
    if needed
Spoon into:
lettuce cups
Garnish with:
tomato wedges
artichoke bottoms
parsley
Serves 4 to 6

CHIFFONADE OF SORREL

Sauté, covered, until liquid
evaporates:
6 to 8 ounces chopped sorrel
2 tablespoons butter
Then add:
2 to 3 tablespoons double cream
salt, pepper and sugar to taste
Use as a garnish for lamb stew,
fillet of sole, veal or sweetbreads,
or cream soups. Use as a nest for
poached eggs, veal or baked
white fish. This chiffonade can
also be served as a vegetable
with buttered bread crumbs or
croûtons.

FROG LEGS WITH SORREL

Cover with:
milk
6 large pairs frog legs
Let stand several hours, drain
and dry thoroughly. Then dust
legs lightly with:
flour, salt, white pepper and
    paprika
Brown lightly on all sides in:
3 tablespoons butter and/or
    olive oil
Remove frog legs from frying pan
and reserve.

To pan add and cook 3 minutes:
1/2 pound mushrooms, thinly
    sliced
4 tablespoons finely chopped
    onion
Add and cook 3 minutes, adding
more butter or oil if needed:
2 ounces chopped sorrel
2 tablespoons finely chopped
    shallots
1/2 teaspoon finely chopped
    garlic
Deglaze with:
6 to 8 tablespoons white wine
Cook rapidly to reduce by half.
Then lower heat and add:
4 tablespoons each creamy milk
    and chicken stock
Cook and stir until smooth and
season to taste with:
lemon juice
salt and freshly ground white
    pepper
Return frog legs to pan, cover
and cook 8 minutes, or until
legs are tender. Do not overcook.
Add more creamy milk or stock
if needed and adjust seasonings.
Serve on toast, with
sprinkling of:
finely chopped parsley
finely chopped chives
Serves 4

SCALLOPS AND HAM IN SORREL SAUCE

Marinate 20 minutes in:
2 tablespoons lemon juice
**1 pound scallops, halved or
    quartered if large**
Drain and dry thoroughly. Set
aside. Sauté until
soft but not brown in:
3 tablespoons butter
**5 tablespoons finely chopped
    onion**
Add and cook 3 minutes:
6 ounces ham, diced
1/2 pound mushrooms, sliced
**3 tablespoons chopped spring
    onions and tops**
1 garlic clove, finely chopped
Push aside and add to frying pan:
1 tablespoon olive oil
Dredge scallops with:
flour seasoned with white pepper
Raise heat and sauté scallops,
turning often, 3 minutes. Add
and cook and stir just until
thickened:
6 to 8 tablespoons dry white wine

Then add:
5 tablespoons creamy milk
**about 3 ounces chopped
    sorrel**
Cook and stir just until blended.
Do not overcook or scallops will
toughen. Sauce should be slightly
thickened but not stiff. Adjust
seasonings, adding creamy milk
if too thick, and transfer to
6 lightly buttered ramekins or
scallop shells. Sprinkle with:
3 to 4 tablespoons grated Gruyère
Dot with:
2 tablespoons butter
Bake in 400° oven 10 minutes
or until bubbly and slightly
browned.
Serves 6

TURKEY AND HEARTS OF PALM WITH SORREL

Arrange in shallow baking dish:
**6 large slices cooked white meat
    of turkey, cut in julienne strips**
3 hard-boiled eggs, sliced
Drain, slice across in 1/2-inch
pieces, and arrange between
turkey and eggs:
**1 large can hearts of palm (about
    30 ounces)**
Melt until bubbly:
4 tablespoons butter

Add and cook until it changes
color:
**6 to 8 ounces chopped
    sorrel**
Sprinkle with:
5 tablespoons flour
Cook and stir 3 minutes and
gradually add:
**1/2 pint each rich turkey or
    chicken stock and creamy milk
    or top of the milk**
Cook and stir until smooth and
thickened.
Season to taste with:
salt
freshly ground white pepper
paprika
Pour over turkey and arrange
on top:
1 2-ounce jar red peppers, drained
Sprinkle with:
**generous 1 ounce coarse bread
    crumbs**
Dot with:
2 tablespoons butter
Bake in 350° oven 15 to 20 minutes or until heated through.
Serves 6

Spearmint

(Mentha spicata)

SPEARMINT
Mentha spicata
Creeping perennial rootstock
1 to 2 feet in height
Fast grower
Propagate from cuttings or division
Sun
Hardy
Leaves eaten
Flowers in summer
Purple flowers

Since the time of the ancients, spearmint has been prized both for its medicinal properties and refreshing fragrance. In Biblical times it was so highly valued that it was the medium of payment of tithes by the Pharisees and its fragrance was so honored that it was strewn on the floors of temples dedicated to the Lord. Pliny writes in the first century of its ability to stimulate the mind and the appetite for food. In ancient England, mint was said to have a fragrance that "rejoiceth the heart of man" and inhalation of it was said to be "comfortable for the head and memory." Its addition to foods as a flavoring and as a garnish has long been practised, and today it is also used in a variety of commercial ways—in cough drops, toothpaste and even cigarettes.

Spearmint, with its pear-shaped, purple flower heads and aromatic, green leaves, has for centuries grown wild from the eastern Mediterranean to England's hedgerows. More recently it has gained favor as a ground cover (if repeatedly trimmed and thinned severely before it becomes rampant). With good, semi-shaded, moist soil, propagation is easy, whether by division of roots in autumn and spring, cuttings in the summer, or sowing seeds. Little cultivation is required. Only snails and slugs in early spring are a problem, though occasionally soil-borne diseases will kill established plantings. Available variegated forms are not usually as flavorful as common spearmint.

High in vitamins A and C, fresh and fragrant spearmint adds coolness to a large variety of foods. Cut young leaves at any time and always use them fresh except in areas where mint dies down in the winter. The leaves can then be frozen or dried for winter use. Frequent clipping of the leaves of the plant will encourage healthy, steady growth. Most common mints may be substituted for spearmint, but they are not so flavorful.

SERVING HINTS

• Spearmint leaves can be used whole, candied or plain, as a garnish for fruit drinks, iced tea, juleps and desserts.

• Chopped leaves are good in a variety of salads: coleslaw; tossed salad with chives and celery; orange sections and onion slices; beetroot or cauliflower, chives and parsley; fruit, especially apple; and *tabbouleh,* the traditional Middle Eastern salad made with bulghur (cracked wheat) softened in cold water.

• Add chopped leaves to vegetable dishes: new potatoes and peas, carrots or sliced tomatoes, or when cooking spinach or courgettes.

• Add chopped mint to a breadcrumb coating for meats and chops.

• To make a butter sauce for basting fish, lamb or veal, combine 2 tablespoons butter, 1 tablespoon chopped mint, salt, pepper and lemon juice to taste.

• Add chopped leaves to yoghurt and honey dressing for salad.

• Fold chopped mint into sour cream and serve a dab on chilled cream of pea soup or hot meat broth.

• Combine with cucumbers and yoghurt to garnish a variety of cold soups, or to serve as a salad.

• Add chopped leaves to marinades, cake icings, orange or lime ice, cottage cheese to accompany fruit salad or compote, pastry for quiche, nutmeg-seasoned creamed spinach, fish cakes, beef broth, shredded onion sauce for braised duck and mustard sauce for meat.

• To make vinegar, steep whole mint sprigs 3 days in white vinegar, discarding old ones each day and replacing them with new sprigs.

• Mint also makes a delicious jelly, or tea. Prepare tea the Moroccan way—lots of fresh leaves and heavy with sugar.

Spearmint

LAHMAJOON

Dissolve until bubbly in:

4 tablespoons lukewarm water
1 tablespoon dry yeast
1/2 teaspoon sugar

Stir in:

1/4 pint milk
2 tablespoons corn oil
1/2 teaspoon salt
4 tablespoons finely chopped
  spearmint

Beat in:

8 ounces unbleached flour

Turn out on floured board and knead at least 10 minutes until smooth and elastic, using flour as needed to keep from sticking. Place in oiled bowl, turn to coat with oil, cover with tea towel and let rise in warm place 1 hour or until double in size.

Combine:

1 pound lean minced lamb
1 large onion, finely chopped
6 tablespoons finely chopped
  spearmint
3 to 4 tablespoons finely chopped
  parsley
1/2 teaspoon finely chopped
  garlic
4 tablespoons finely chopped
  green pepper
3 tablespoons tomato paste
3/4 teaspoon salt
1/4 teaspoon each freshly ground
  black pepper, cumin and
  chili powder

Sauté a small amount and adjust seasonings. Divide dough into 8 balls and let rest 5 minutes. On floured board roll each ball into a thin round about 7 inches in diameter. Spread lamb filling on each round and place on lightly oiled baking sheet. Bake in 400° oven 15 minutes or until edges are puffed and golden. Serve immediately. Make 8 lahmajoons

MINT ASPIC

Sprinkle over:
2 tablespoons cold water
1 tablespoon lemon juice
1-1/2 teaspoons gelatine
Dissolve mixture in:
6 tablespoons hot water
In blender purée:
6 to 8 tablespoons water
about 3 ounces chopped
   spearmint
2 tablespoons sugar
1/4 teaspoon salt
Strain, if desired, and add to
gelatine mixture. Line bottoms of
6 small round moulds with some
of the gelatine mixture to make
layer about 1/4 inch deep. Chill
until set. Place in center of each
mould:

1 cantaloupe ball
Arrange in flower fashion around
each ball:
chrysanthemum petals
Carefully pour in enough of the
gelatine without disturbing pattern
almost to cover. Chill until set
and pour in rest of the gelatine.
Chill until firm and unmould.
Serve as accompaniment to
lamb roast.
Serves 6

SPEARMINT TARTS

Thaw in refrigerator overnight:
about 12 ounces puff pastry
Combine and set aside:
3 ounces soft brown sugar
8 ounces raisins, finely chopped
4 ounces finely chopped
   spearmint
Roll puff pastry thinly, a portion
at a time, and cut into 4-inch
rounds. Lower into tart tins and
refrigerate while working with
rest of pastry, making 12 tart
shells in all. Line pastry-filled
tart tins with greaseproof paper
and fill with:
dry beans or rice
Refrigerate 30 minutes and then
place in 450° oven. Lower heat
to 425° and bake 15 minutes.
Remove beans or rice and greaseproof
paper. Cool and fill with reserved
mint filling. Dot each tart with:
1/2 teaspoon butter
Bake in 375° oven 10 minutes
until filling is heated through and
edges of pastry are golden.
Remove to rack and cool slightly.
Garnish each tart with:
tiny sprig of spearmint
Serve as dessert or with after-
noon tea.
Makes 12

Strawberry

(*Fragaria vesca* and cultivars)

STRAWBERRY
Fragaria vesca and cultivars
Perennial ground cover
To 8 to 10 inches in height
Fast grower
Propagate from runners
Sun
Hardy
Berries eaten
Flowers in early spring
Harvest in late spring and early summer
White flowers, red berries

The origin of the strawberry is lost in history, but even the ancients wrote of it. Ovid and Pliny paid tribute to this unusual fruit. And in his third *Eclogue*, Virgil wrote: "Ye boys that gather flowers and strawberries/ Lo, hid within the grass an adder lies."

London street vendors, John Lidgate wrote in 1430, cried, "Strabery ripe!" And according to privy purse expense records, Henry VIII paid 10 shillings for a "pottle of strawberries," a small basket suitable only for small berries. The small, sweet *fraises des bois*, wild strawberries, are still sold today in European markets. But in the early 14th century, the French transplanted wild strawberries from the woods into their gardens and found strawberries could be grown to the size of blackberries. Hybridizers have been breeding for size ever since and have developed strains as large as plums (along with everblooming varieties and some that ripen white), thereby contributing mightily to the strawberry's popularity.

The strawberry was developed by various men through the ages. But no single step forward has the excitement and history of the first giant step—the marriage in France of two New World varieties which became the pollen parents of the lush berries of today. This occurred during the reign of Louis XIV, who knowing his regency hold on the Spanish throne was unpopular and short-lived, sent a Frenchman, Lt. Colonel Frezier, to spy on the fortifications of Chile and Peru. Frezier, disguised as a merchant, studied more than fortifications. He discovered exceptional strawberries, *F. chilensis,* with as long a history as the European varieties, and brought back plants to France. It turned out they were all female and, lacking a pollen parent, could not produce the spectacular fruit Frezier had observed. However, when planted near a North American native, *F. virginiana,* the Chilean strawberry thrived and produced large berries like those we know today.

No one is sure how strawberries were named; theories suggest it's because they ripen along with straw or because they strew out their runners along the soil.

A sunny location, good sandy soil with plenty of humus and adequate moisture are ideal for strawberries. Heavier soils should not be overwatered. Buy plants or snip runners from a friend's plants. Plant with crowns just above the soil in early spring or late summer. Late summer planting will enable settling in over the winter and perhaps a small fruit crop the first year. However, if the plants are not well established, remove the first flower crop to allow them to build up strength before fruiting. Feed in spring and late summer. Space new planting widely (two feet apart) so that runners can be arranged to root in between. Remove some of the runners if overcrowding occurs. Straw under the berries protects the fruit and promotes even ripening. Container planting adds interest; the variety Sonjana can be trained to climb on a trellis.

If red core rots the center of your plants and the leaves turn yellow, replace them. Red spider mites and aphids should be controlled. It's advisable to replace parent plants every three or four years with runners they've produced.

Strawberries are best eaten right from the plant with a bit of sugar added if desired. But your strawberry plants may produce a prolific enough crop to have plenty of berries for experimentation in the kitchen. The berries are ripe when they are an even clear-red color. Pick gently from the plant and, being careful not to bruise them, wash well and remove the caps.

Strawberry

SERVING HINTS

- For dessert, dip whole strawberries in Cointreau and then in powdered sugar, or combine with sliced almonds and a complementary cordial.
- Coat strawberries with fritter batter (page 30) and deep fry.
- Fold into tapioca pudding, chill and serve with whipped cream.
- Encase small whole strawberries in a pastry ball and bake until golden.

- Form cantaloupe balls, combine with strawberries and marinate in Port. Return to cantaloupe shells if desired, chill and serve.
- Combine diced strawberries with orange sections or mix with bananas and orange juice.
- Make a cream cheese ring and fill the center with fresh whole strawberries.

- Halved berries may be added to scrambled eggs just before serving or, at the last minute, to cucumbers dressed with sour cream.

STRAWBERRY LEAVES

The leaves of the strawberry plant are edible and are high in vitamin C and iron, as are the berries. For a different beverage, make strawberry tea with the fresh leaves.

MIXED FRUIT JAM

Have ready:
**2 cups each raspberries, red or
  black currants, strawberries
  and pitted cherries**
5 cups sugar
In a large pan layer the fruit,
sprinkling each layer with sugar.
Let stand 3 hours, shaking pan
occasionally. Then bring to the
boil and boil 20 minutes or until
thickened. Pour into hot sterilized jars, seal and store in a cool,
dry place.

OYSTERS WITH STRAWBERRIES

Sauté 2 minutes in:
4 tablespoons butter
**6 to 8 tablespoons finely
  chopped garlic chive bulbs,
  white and a little green of
  stem (page 62)**
Add and sauté quickly until
edges curl:
**10 ounces oysters, drained and
  cut up if large**
Season while cooking with:
**1/4 teaspoon each salt and
  freshly ground white pepper**
Remove oysters with slotted
spoon and sprinkle pan with:
2 tablespoons flour
Cook and stir until flour starts
to brown. Reduce heat. Blend in
4 tablespoons dry white wine
1/4 pint creamy milk
**about 2 ounces finely chopped
  nasturtium leaves**
Stir *constantly* until thickened.
Return oysters to pan and
reheat. Gently stir in:
4 ounces strawberries, halved
Adjust seasonings and serve
immediately in:
4 baked puff pastry shells
Garnish with:
whole strawberries
Serves 4

STRAWBERRY ROSE ICE

Purée in blender:
2 cups sliced strawberries
1/2 cup rose sugar (page 28)
1 teaspoon rose water
Blend in until smooth:
3/4 pint plain yoghurt
Pour into ice tray and freeze until
almost frozen. Then transfer to
deep bowl and beat over ice until
smooth. Fold in:
1 stiffly beaten egg white
Freeze only until firm but not
solid and serve scoops with fruit
salad or as dessert garnished with:
whole strawberries
mint sprigs
Serves 8

Swiss Chard

(Beta vulgaris and cultivars)

It is hard to realize that Swiss chard and beetroot are members of the same family. Chard has been used as a potherb in Europe since the beginning of recorded food plant history. In the fourth century, Aristotle wrote about the red chard and Theophrastus mentioned the light and dark-green varieties. In the 16th century a Swiss botanist described the yellow form; hence, the plant came to be called Swiss chard. It grew wild in and around the Mediterranean Sea, but was introduced over the centuries to many parts of Europe. Although today more compact and fleshier-leaved varieties have been selected, they are not much different from the wild kinds eaten by the Romans.

Sow seeds outdoors in March in shallow drills a half inch deep in sunny or slightly shaded, fertile, well-drained soil. When the plants are two to three inches in height, thin them out to 12 inches apart or transplant them to appropriate spots in the decorative garden. Keep weed-free, and protect from slugs and snails. By mid-summer the first leaves will be ready to be cut, and cutting can continue until autumn. Cutting regularly will encourage the plant to produce more young growths from the center. Red chard, especially, can be effectively used to add color and interest to the summer garden.

Swiss chard can be cooked in almost any manner that spinach is cooked. Red chard stems and ribs of mature leaves are tougher than white ones though, and do not cook as rapidly. Once cooked, it may be necessary to remove the ribs before chopping the leaves for a particular recipe. Tender young leaves need no moisture in cooking other than the water that clings after washing. One pound fresh chard yields approximately one cup firmly packed cooked and chopped chard. Swiss chard is good flavored with rosemary.

PEASANT SOUP

Combine:
**1/2 pound each minced beef and
veal**
**6 to 8 tablespoons finely chopped
cooked Swiss chard**
**2 tablespoons finely chopped
parsley**
**1 tablespoon freshly grated
lemon peel**
**4 tablespoons finely chopped
onion**
1 garlic clove, finely chopped
1/2 teaspoon salt
**1/4 teaspoon each freshly ground
black pepper and freshly
grated nutmeg**
2 tablespoons bread crumbs
1 egg, beaten
Chill, then form into 4 dozen
1-1/4-inch balls. Sauté slowly to
cook through on all sides in:
1 tablespoon butter
Bring to boil:
5 pints chicken stock
Add and boil slowly 5 minutes
meatballs and:
**about 3 ounces coarsely chopped
Swiss chard**

Beat well:
2 eggs
**2 tablespoons each water
.water and grated Parmesan cheese**
Stirring constantly, slowly pour
egg mixture into soup. Cook and
stir until eggs are set. Serve immediately with:
extra grated cheese
Accompany with garlic French
bread and green salad.
Serves 8 for main meal

SWISS CHARD SALAD MOULD

Remove tough stems from:
2 pounds Swiss chard
Wash and place in heavy saucepan.
Cover and cook until tender.
Drain thoroughly and chop,
removing any stems that did not
cook evenly. (There should be
about 1-1/2 pints firmly packed.)
Set aside.
Soften in:
1/4 pint cold water
2 envelopes gelatine
Dissolve in:
1/2 pint hot water
Then add:
2 to 3 tablespoons sugar
3/4 teaspoon salt
4 tablespoons lemon juice

Chill until starting to set. Beat
until light and fluffy; fold in
reserved chard and:
5 tablespoons mayonnaise
**8 ounces drained, creamed
cottage cheese**
**5 tablespoons very finely chopped
celery**
Pour into lightly oiled 2-1/2-pint
mould, cover and chill until firm,
6 hours or more. Turn out onto
chilled platter. Surround with
lettuce cups and decorate with:
sieved hard-boiled egg
celery curls
Serve with light crackers or
melba toast.
Serves 8

Swiss Chard

SWISS CHARD FRITTERS

Remove tough stems from:
3/4 to 1 pound Swiss chard
Wash and place in heavy saucepan.
Cover and cook until tender.
Remove cover and cook all moisture away. Cool and chop
finely. Measure 1 cup firmly
packed and set aside.
In blender combine:
3/4 cup milk
1/2 cup flour
1 egg
**1/4 teaspoon each salt, sugar
    and finely chopped rosemary**
**1/8 teaspoon freshly ground
    black pepper**

Stir in chard (do not blend).
Drop mixture by spoonfuls into:
hot butter
Make a cake about 3-1/2 inches
in diameter. Brown both sides,
adding butter as needed. Just
before serving top each fritter
with:
browned butter
Serve as accompaniment to
Wiener schnitzel or other meat
dish.
Makes approximately 16 fritters

SERVING HINTS

• When stir frying or butter
steaming chard sauté the stems
with a little finely chopped onion
and/or garlic to precook them
before adding the tender leaves.
• The stems can be left whole,
dipped in batter (page 30) and
deep fried.
• Add chopped, cooked chard
to frittatas, or chop very finely
for adding to a soufflé.
• The torn leaves can be added
to lentil soup for the last few minutes of cooking time.

Thyme

(Thymus vulgaris and *Thymus* x *citriodorus)*

Of the hundred species of *Thymus, T. vulgaris* and *T.* x *citriodorus* are most popular for culinary purposes. Thyme's early Greek use was as a fumigant, simply crushed, or as an incense. Its strong odor was associated with courage because of its invigorative properties. In southern France wild thyme is the symbol of extreme republicanism. No wonder it is used in the kitchen to perk up so many dishes.

Thyme honey is renowned; Romans flavored their cheeses with thyme. It has also been used to cure sciatica, headaches, rheumatism and intestinal worms. Thymol, distilled oil of thyme or its synthetic equivalent, is a powerful antiseptic, deodorant, fungicide and meat preservative; it's useful for cosmetics, to protect linens from insects and for embalming as well.

This versatile little plant makes an ideal border when seeds are planted in March or April either in position or in rows for transplanting later. It likes the sun, requires little water, is amenable to shaping and trimming, and has few enemies.

Lemon-scented thyme *(T.* x *citriodorus)* can be encouraged to thicken by mounding soil around it in the spring and removing rooted-out shoots in autumn. It grows well as a creeping ground cover for rock gardens. While older plants can be divided, new seed sowing every three or four years is easier.

Pleasantly pungent, thyme is one of the most essential of all culinary herbs. A close relative of oregano and sweet marjoram, its variety of flavors—lemon, orange, caraway—will successfully complement a wide array of dishes. As branches come into flower, snip several inch-long young, tender thyme sprigs. Use fresh, or dry or quick freeze them for later use.

THYME
Thymus vulgaris *and*
Thymus x citriodorus
Short-lived, perennial ground cover
1 to 2 feet in height
Fast grower when established
Propagate from seed or cuttings
Sun or light shade
Leaves eaten
Flowers in summer
Blue or violet flowers

Thyme

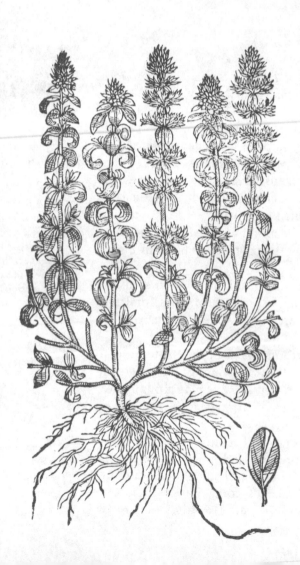

SERVING HINTS

- Use thyme to flavor meats, fish and fish cakes, poultry, croquettes, fricassées, stews, soups, chowders and stuffings.
- Combine with savory and sweet basil in a bouquet garni for roast chicken or turkey, or with parsley, savory and bay for placing in the cavity of a roasting fowl.
- Add thyme to bread, scone and bun doughs, or flavor home-made croûtons with the finely chopped leaves.
- Infuse salad dressing or vinegar with thyme, and sprinkle it on cooked vegetables to enhance their flavor.
- For tea, add 1 tablespoon dried thyme leaves to a cup of hot water. Sweeten with 1 tablespoon honey and add a pinch of salt. This tea is said to be good for hangover sufferers.

POTATO SALAD IN TOMATO CUPS

Cook until soft:
1 pound unpeeled white potatoes
4 large sprigs lemon thyme
1 teaspoon lemon juice
Cool, peel, dice and set aside.
Combine:
4 tablespoons mayonnaise
3 tablespoons garlic olive oil
8 tablespoons (firmly packed)
 finely chopped sorrel
4 tablespoons finely chopped
 parsley
2 tablespoons finely chopped
 garlic chives
6 to 8 ounces diced cooked prawns
 or flaked crab
Toss in potato cubes and season
to taste with:
salt and white pepper
lemon juice
Hollow out:
8 large ripe tomatoes
Salt lightly and tip upside down
for 10 minutes. Chop enough of
the pulp to make a scant 1/2 pint
and add to potatoes. Fill
tomatoes with potato salad and
sprinkle with:
paprika
Garnish with:
lemon wedges
Serves 8

CREAM OF LENTIL SOUP

Sauté until soft in:
2 tablespoons butter
6 tablespoons chopped onion
1 large stalk celery and
 leaves
2 garlic cloves, chopped
Add:
6 ounces lentils
4 large sprigs lemon thyme
1-1/2 pints beef stock
Bring to gentle boil, cover and
simmer 45 minutes or until lentils
are soft. Force through sieve or
food mill. Add:
1/4 pint creamy milk
Season to taste with:
chopped gladiolus petals
salt
freshly ground white pepper
If too thick, thin with:
stock or creamy milk
Top with:
chopped gladiolus petals
Serves 4 to 6

VEAL ROLLS

Pound until paper thin:
6 large thin slices veal (about
 3 ounces each)
Sprinkle each slice with:
1/2 teaspoon finely chopped
 thyme or lemon thyme
freshly ground white pepper
Place on each slice:
2 or 3 slices prosciutto
Cover with:
thinly sliced Mozzarella or
 mild Cheddar cheese
about 2 tablespoons chopped
 cooked sweetbreads (page 178)
Roll tightly and tie in 3 or 4
places. Coat rolls with:
flour
salt and white pepper
marjoram
Brown on all sides in:
2 tablespoons each garlic olive
 oil and butter
Deglaze frying pan with:
scant 1/2 pint dry white wine
Cover tightly, lower heat and
cook until rolls are tender, adding last 10 minutes if desired:
1/2 pound small whole mush-
 rooms
more wine
Remove rolls to heated platter.
Surround with steamed asparagus
and mashed potatoes and pour
pan juices over all.
Serves 6

Thyme

SWEETBREADS

Cover with ice water, changing water twice, for 30 minutes:
2 pounds veal sweetbreads
Drain and place in saucepan with a mixture of:
3/4 pint dry white wine
2 large carrots, cut up
2 stalks celery with leaves, cut up
2 medium onions, quartered
8 sprigs thyme or lemon thyme
6 parsley sprigs
1 teaspoon salt
14 peppercorns, lightly crushed
Barely cover with
boiling water
Bring to gentle boil, cover and simmer 10 to 15 minutes depending upon size of sweetbreads. Turn once. Remove from heat, tip lid and cool. Cover and refrigerate overnight to blend flavors. Remove sweetbreads, trim fat and membrane and pull apart into pieces. Strain cooking liquid and reserve. If freezing, place sweetbreads in jar and pour strained liquid in up to 1 inch from top of jar. Cover. Use in following recipe or any recipe calling for sweetbreads.

SWEETBREAD/MUSHROOM RAMEKINS

Beat together:
1 egg
2 to 3 teaspoons dry sherry or lemon juice
Combine:
2 ounces bread crumbs
1 tablespoon very finely chopped thyme or lemon thyme
1/4 teaspoon each salt, paprika and freshly ground white pepper
Break into small pieces:
1-1/2 pounds cooked sweetbreads (preceding)
Dip pieces in beaten egg and then coat thoroughly with crumbs. Refrigerate at least 1 hour.
Heat:
1 tablespoon each butter and garlic olive oil
Brown sweetbreads, not touching, on all sides, adding more butter and oil as needed. Remove to 5 or 6 buttered ramekins. In same pan, quickly sauté until golden:
3/4 pound mushrooms, sliced
Season while they are cooking with:
1/4 teaspoon salt
1/8 teaspoon freshly ground white pepper
Sprinkle with:
3 tablespoons flour
1 teaspoon very finely chopped thyme or lemon thyme
Cook and stir for 3 minutes and gradually add:
generous 1/2 pint stock reserved from cooking sweetbreads
Stir constantly until smooth and thickened. (Be sure flour does not cling to mushroom slices.) Add and blend well:
5 tablespoons double cream
Cook and stir a few minutes to thicken again. Pour over and around sweetbreads in ramekins and tuck in sauce:
36 red dessert grapes, halved and seeded
Bake in 350°oven 15 minutes or until bubbly and heated through. If making ahead, refrigerate and add 10 minutes or so to cooking time. Just before serving sprinkle with:
finely chopped parsley
Serves 5 to 6

Violet
& Garden Pansy

(Viola odorata and
Viola x *wittrockiana* and cultivars)

VIOLET AND GARDEN PANSY
<u>Viola</u> <u>odorata</u> *and*
<u>Viola</u> *x* <u>wittrockiana</u> *and cultivars*
Annual or short-lived perennial
ground cover, or suitable
for bedding
To 8 to 10 inches in height
Propagate from seed
Sun; light shade in warmer areas
Hardy, except in coldest areas
Flowers and leaves eaten
Flowers in spring, summer and
autumn, depending on when
seed is sown
Various colors

Called, among other names, "Three faces in one head," "Kit run the streets," "Herb trinity" and "Heartsease," pansies found many uses in medicine. In his herbal, Culpeper wrote that a strong decoction or syrup of the herb and flowers is an excellent cure for venereal disease, the spirit of it is excellent for convulsions in children and a remedy for falling sickness, inflammation of the lungs and breasts, pleurisy, scabs, itch etc., and the flowers are cooling, emollient and cathartic.

Unlike its wilder cousin, the violet, the pansy has enjoyed 150 years of hybridizing by enthusiastic gardeners. Over 400 named varieties were being offered for sale by 1835, with special rules promulgated for pansy judging—flat, circular flowers of at least two inches in diameter, etc. The best varieties could only be propagated by cuttings until American hybridizers later produced seeds that uniformly produced desired sizes and colors.

Well-worked soil in areas with lots of light, but not too much direct sun, should be earmarked for planting out pansies. Seeds must be sown in summer for planting out in autumn, or in early January for spring planting. Sow the seed sparsely, barely covered, and keep in a temperature of 60°F. (The temperature requirement may necessitate sowing only in the summer.) When plants develop, they should be pricked out in larger flats with three-inch spacing and allowed to mature. Autumn planting is best done by mid-September so the plants will have time to establish themselves before winter sets in. To ensure prolific blooming, remove dead flowers.

Thoughts of sweetness, innocence and gentleness come to mind when one thinks of violets and pansies. High in vitamins A and C and in iron, the flowers and the leaves are edible and of delicate flavor. The pansy, however, is stronger in flavor. To prepare them for the kitchen, pick the flowers before the sun is on them, wash gently but thoroughly and pat dry with a light hand. They may be dried, though their appealing texture is lost in the process.

SERVING HINTS

• Long admired for their culinary elegance, candied violets and pansies make a beautiful garnish for desserts or can be folded into a dessert soufflé.

• The flowers can be used in making flavored syrups and honeys, or can be added to preserves.

• Make violet or pansy tea by using fresh or dried flowers and leaves if desired, and let steep about 5 minutes.

• The leaves make an attractive base for holding moulds or garnishes, and the flowers can be used as a garnish for cold fruit soups with or without a dollop of sour cream.

• Make a pansy or violet leaf chiffonade or use as a potherb with other greens.

VIOLET SALAD

Wash and discard tough leaves and stems:

1 pound young spinach leaves
Dry, wrap in tea towel and refrigerate until ready to serve.
Toss together and refrigerate:
6 ounces mushrooms, sliced
1 teaspoon each lemon juice and garlic olive oil
cayenne pepper and powdered oregano to taste

Just before serving toss mushrooms and spinach with:
6 tablespoons garlic olive oil
3 tablespoons each soy sauce and lemon juice
2 ounces water chestnuts, sliced
2 hard-boiled eggs, chopped
1 ounce croûtons
salt and pepper to taste
Arrange on top:
1 cup violet flowers crisped in ice water and dried
Serve immediately
Serves 8 to 10

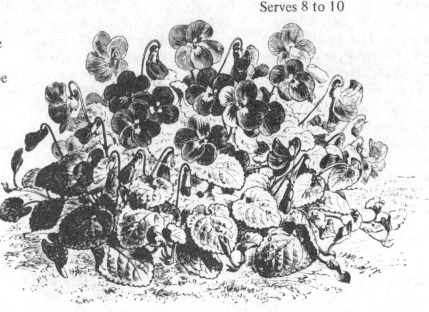

Violet & Garden Pansy

SALTIMBOCCA

Pound between sheets of grease-proof paper until paper thin:
16 thin slices veal
Season with:
freshly ground black pepper
Place on half the slices:
2 slices prosciutto, or
1 thin slice of ham or lightly salted rare roast beef
Sprinkle each with:
1 to 2 teaspoons very finely chopped pansy or violet petals
Top with rest of veal and press down firmly. Trim overlapping edges. Cut in halves or thirds and weave a toothpick in each piece to secure.
Melt until foamy in a frying pan:
3 tablespoons butter
Over medium high heat sauté the veal, without letting pieces touch, 4 minutes per side or until tender. Do not overcook. Add more butter as needed. Remove to heated platter and keep warm. Deglaze pan with:
3 to 4 tablespoons Marsala or white wine

Do not allow to boil. Stir in:
1 tablespoon soft butter
Pour over veal and serve immediately sprinkled with:
finely chopped parsley
paprika
Garnish with:
lemon slices or wedges
Serves 4 to 6

VARIATION WITH CHICKEN BREASTS

Partially freeze boned breasts and with very sharp knife split each breast in half lengthwise to make thin slices. Pound and proceed as directed with veal. Sauté only 2 minutes per side.

PANSY HONEY CUSTARD

Combine and heat 15 minutes in double boiler:
5 tablespoons honey
3 tablespoons very finely chopped pansy leaves and flowers
Place in covered jars and let mellow 3 days.
Scald:
3/4 pint milk
Add prepared pansy honey and:
1/4 teaspoon salt
Heat until honey is dissolved.
Beat 1/4 pint of the hot milk mixture into:
3 eggs, beaten
Beat this back into rest of the hot milk and pour into 6 lightly buttered custard cups. Sprinkle each with:
freshly grated nutmeg to taste
Place in pan half filled with water and bake in 375° oven 30 minutes or until toothpick inserted in center comes out clean. Garnish with:
fresh violet or pansy flowers
Serves 6

Recommended Nurseries

Below is a list of some specialist nurseries and seed houses from which plants, seeds and/or cuttings may be ordered by post. All have catalogues.

ASPARAGUS
A. R. Paske & Co. Ltd.,
Regal Lodge, Kentford,
Newmarket, Suffolk

BLUEBERRIES
James Trehane & Sons Ltd.,
Stapehill Road, Hampreston,
near Wimborne, Dorset

BULBS (INCLUDING LILIES)
P. de Jager & Sons Ltd.,
The Nurseries,
Marden, Kent

CHRYSANTHEMUMS
Elm House Nurseries Ltd.,
Walpole St. Peter,
Wisbech, Cambs.

SOFT FRUIT
Ken Muir,
Honeypot Fruit Farm,
Clacton-on-Sea, Essex

Also from Tree and Shrub Nurseries

TOP FRUIT
Blackmoor Nurseries,
Blackmoor,
Liss, Hants.
Also from Tree and Shrub Nurseries

HERBS
A. & E. Evett,
Ashfield Herb Nurseries,
Hinstock, Market Drayton,
Shropshire

The Herb Farm,
Broad Oak Road,
Canterbury, Kent

Also from Seedsmen

ROSES
John Mattock,
The Rose Nurseries,
Nuneham Courtenay, Oxford

TREES AND SHRUBS (ALSO FRUIT)
Hillier & Sons,
Winchester, Hants

Notcutts Nurseries Ltd.,
Woodbridge, Suffolk

John Scott & Co.,
The Royal Nurseries,
Nerriott, Somerset

VEGETABLE & FLOWER SEEDS (INCLUDING HERBS)
Samuel Dobie & Sons Ltd.,
Upper Dee Mills,
Llangollen, Clwyd.

Sutton Seeds Ltd.,
Reading, Berks.

Thompson & Morgan Ltd.,
London Road, Ipswich, Suffolk

W. & J. Unwin Ltd.,
Histon, Cambridge

Glossary

Annual: A plant which grows, flowers and produces seed, completing its life cycle within one year.

Basal-Plate Root Rot: A fungus disease which rots the basal plate (the base of a bulb), and sometimes the entire bulb. Badly diseased bulbs should be discarded.

Biennial: A plant requiring two seasons to complete its life cycle.

Black Spot: A fungus disease which produces black spots on the leaves of a plant, and eventually, complete loss of foliage. A common enemy of the rose.

Chocolate Spot: A fungus disease which produces chocolate-brown spots on the foliage.

Common Name: A name given a plant other than the correct botanical name. This name can vary from region to region.

Conifer: A tree that produces woody cones containing naked seeds. Firs and pines are examples.

Crown Rot: A fungus disease, especially affecting ornamentals, which first yellows the shoots and then causes rapid decay of the crown (portion of the plant at soil level from which the stem rises).

Cultivar: A plant that has been selected and propagated, and is generally superior in one or more ways to the species.

Deciduous: Term applied to a plant that sheds its leaves in the winter.

Double-digging: Term used to describe digging two spade depths deep, thus creating a large volume of loose, aerated soil for roots to spread and better absorption of moisture and food.

Drill Rows: Term used to describe the sowing of seeds in evenly spaced rows.

Espalier: Term meaning to train the main shoot vertically and the lateral branches in a specific manner in tiers parallel to the ground.

Evergreen: A plant which retains its foliage from season to season. In time, the leaves are shed, but it is such a gradual process that their absence goes unnoticed.

Eye: An isolated bud removed from the parent plant for propagation.

Family: A group of plants containing varying numbers of genera, the members of which have the number and the placement of flower parts in common.

Flat: A shallow box, usually wood, used for sowing seeds, or to which seedlings, once large enough, are transferred before transplanting.

Genus: A subdivision of a plant family containing groups of species which have common characteristics.

Herbaceous: Term applied to plants which die down at the end of a growing season.

Hybrid: The result of crossing two different parent plants, the progeny being different from either parent.

Latin Name: Refers to the correct botanical name of a plant by which it is known throughout the world.

Nursery Rows: Small plants are planted in "nursery rows" until they reach sufficient size to plant in a final location.

Perennial: A plant with a life span of more than two years.

Potting on: The moving of a plant from a small-size pot to a large one.

Pre-emergent Herbicide: A chemical which inhibits the germination of seed.

Pricking out: The replanting of seedlings from where they have germinated to a flat or container where they can develop until large enough to plant.

Red Core: A disease which attacks strawberries, causing the center of the root to have a red core.

Species: A subdivision of a genus containing plants with characteristics in common.

Specimen Plant: A plant which is allowed to develop in isolation without competition from other plants.

Standard and Half Standard: A tree trained so that the trunk grows erect to the desired height before the branches are allowed to form a head. A standard is from six to eight feet in height; a half standard, from three to four.

Terminal Bud: The bud at the apex of a shoot.

Water Shoots: Vigorous shoots generally arising from a cut branch. They are normally upright and cannot form the main structure of a tree.

Index

HORTICULTURAL INDEX

Index

RECIPE INDEX

Index

Index

Index

Index

in potato salad in tomato cups, 177
in primrose leaves with sorrel, 133
scallops and ham in sorrel
    sauce, 163
serving hints, 161
sorrel-celeriac salad, 162
turkey and hearts of palm with
    sorrel, 163

Soups
blueberry soup, 79
chestnut soup, 57
cold corn and courgette chowder,
    103
cold cream cheese soup, 50
cream of lentil soup, 177
cream of parsley soup, 129
elderberry soup, 91
peasant soup, 173
root borshch, 130
rose hip soup, 151
shellfish soup, 115
tortilla soup, 85
Spaghetti with Chive Sauce, 64
Spearmint, 165-167
lahmajoon, 166
mint aspic, 167
serving hints, 165
spearmint tarts, 167
Spiced Crab Apples, 75
Spiced Oranges, 114
Squid, Primrose Stuffed, 134
Strawberry, 170-171
mixed fruit jam, 171
oysters with strawberries, 171
serving hints, 170

strawberry leaves, 170
strawberry rose ice, 171
Stock, To Infuse, 28
Stuffing, Blueberry, for Poultry, 79
Stuffing, Couscous, for Poultry, 151
Stuffing, Currant, for Goose, 82
Sweet and Sour Chicken, 60
Sweetbread/Mushroom Ramekins, 178
Sweetbreads, 178
Swiss Chard, 172-174
peasant soup, 173
in pork patties, 154
in primrose leaf green noodles
    (variation), 135
serving hints, 174
Swiss chard fritters, 174
Swiss chard salad mould, 173
Syrup, To Make, 27

Tea, To Make, 28
Thyme, 176-178
in asparagus casserole, 39
in asparagus purée, 37
in busecca, 158
cream of lentil soup, 177
potato salad in tomato cups, 177
in rabbit pie, 70
serving hints, 176
sweetbread/mushroom ramekins,
    178
sweetbreads, 178
veal rolls, 177
in venison fondue, 111
in venison stew, 85
Tortilla Soup, 85
Trifle, 108

Turkey
calendula ramekin, 50
turkey and crab apple crêpes, 73
turkey and hearts of palm with
    sorrel, 163
turkey cutlets, 42
turkey rice casserole, 53

Veal
artichoke and sweetbread pie, 35
peasant soup, 173
saltimbocca, 182
sweetbread/mushroom ramekins,
    178
sweetbreads, 178
veal rolls, 177
Vegetable Spaghetti, Steamed, 111
Venison
cabbage rolls, 110
venison fondue, 111
venison sage sausage, 158
venison stew, 85
Vinegar, To Make Flavored, 28
Violet, 181-182
in blueberry soup, 79
in blueberry tortoni, 79
in Concord grape pudding, 108
in pansy honey custard, 182
saltimbocca, 182
serving hints, 181
in trifle, 108
violet salad, 181
Violet Water, 28-29

Wild Boar Chops, 60
Won Ton Rolls, 115

191

Biographical Data

JOHN E. BRYAN

John E. Bryan is currently Director of the Strybing Arboretum and Botanic Gardens in San Francisco's Golden Gate Park. But his career as a horticulturist spans two continents. Born in 1931 in England, he graduated from the Royal Botanic Garden in Edinburgh in 1955, and did post-graduate work at the Royal Horticultural Society Gardens, Wisley (on a scholarship given only once in three years), at the Hague in Holland and in France from 1955 through 1958. Upon completing his studies, he managed the herbaceous and perennial nursery of Vilmorin in Paris. In 1961 he came to the United States and became sales manager of Jan de Graaff's Oregon Bulb Farms. He has travelled extensively throughout the United States and Canada, visiting botanical gardens and nurseries and giving lectures. John Bryan now lectures on many horticultural subjects and his articles have been published in numerous magazines and professional journals in the United States and abroad. He is a contributor to Sunset's latest book on pruning and was general consultant for the book on evergreens in the Time-Life *Encyclopedia of Gardening*.

CORALIE CASTLE

Coralie Castle met John Bryan when she went to the Strybing Arboretum for some advice on an unusual plant in her own very ornamental and highly edible garden. Their mutual interests in food and in gardening led to the collaboration on this book, with John Bryan supplying the horticultural expertise and Mrs. Castle developing the recipes, often using the fruits, flowers, vegetables and herbs from her own large garden. This is her fourth cookbook for 101 Productions. She wrote *Soup* in 1971; followed this in 1972 with *Peasant Cooking of Many Lands*, in a co-authorship with Margaret Gin; and in 1973 produced *Hors d'Oeuvre, Etc.* with Barbara Lawrence. Born and raised in Kenilworth, Illinois, Coralie Castle and her husband Alfred live in Marin County, north of San Francisco.